Love Like Salt

Love Like Salt

A Memoir

Helen Stevenson

virago

VIRAGO

First published in Great Britain in 2016 by Virago Press

1 3 5 7 9 10 8 6 4 2

A CIP catalogue record for this book
is available from the British Library.

ISBN 978-0-349-00779-3

Typeset in Perpetua by M Rules
Printed and bound in Great Britain by
Clays Ltd, St Ives plc

Papers used by Virago are from well-managed forests
and other responsible sources.

MIX
Paper from
responsible sources
FSC
www.fsc.org   FSC® C104740

Virago Press
An imprint of
Little, Brown Book Group
Carmelite House
50 Victoria Embankment
London EC4Y 0DZ

An Hachette UK Company
www.hachette.co.uk

www.virago.co.uk

For Nico, Clara and Verity

Cystic fibrosis is a genetically inherited disease affecting over 70,000 people worldwide, and over 9,000 in the UK alone.

Salt is unable to pass easily from one cell to the next, with the result that the body's balance of salt and water is upset. This leads to a build-up of thick mucus and consequent infections in the body's organs, particularly in the digestive system and lungs. It requires intensive treatment by physiotherapy and medication. Although until relatively recently it was unusual for 'the child whose brow tastes salty when kissed' to survive into adulthood, new treatments have improved the outlook considerably. One day gene therapy may be able to halt the progress of the disease.

The folk tale 'Love Like Salt', given here in its Italian version, appears in oral and written versions all over the world.

A king had three daughters. He called them to him and asked each in turn how much she loved him.

'I love you as much as my eyes,' said the first, and the King was pleased.

'I love you as much as my heart,' said the second, and again the King was pleased.

'I love you as much as salt,' said the third.

At this the King became angry. He banished his youngest daughter from the palace. She wandered in the forest for many months. One day she returned to the palace, where she found work in the kitchen. On the day of the King's birthday she prepared the meat for his table, and the vegetables, and the soup, each without salt. When the King tasted his food he exclaimed, 'It has no flavour at all! Bring me the fool who prepared these saltless dishes for my table!'

When the cook was summoned from the kitchen, the King recognised his daughter. 'Who is the fool now?' he said, and embraced her in sorrow for his cruelty, and in joy at her love for him.

PREFACE

We lived for seven years in a small town in France.

It was not remarkable for its beauty, and therefore did not suffer unduly from it. A wide river ran through it, and for centuries people had made their home there. Sheep and the sun kept the grass on the chalky uplands short-bitten and coarse; the wool was shipped in barges to bigger, busier towns. The local priest deferred to a distant bishop, and even the vegetables were transported to places up- or downstream for sale at market. The postcards in the newsagent showed views of other villages, not this one. With nothing in particular to distinguish it, or thrust it before the world's attention, it had survived amiably, with no starlet pout or hand on hip. You could imagine living well there, unaffected, largely, by fashion or cravings or sudden seismic shifts in world opinion.

I was not born there, nor sent there, but went of my own accord. We were looking for a house in a part of France neither of us knew. I had lived in the Pyrenées Orientales, my husband had grown up partly in Provence. He was twenty years older me, and we had two daughters under six who had been born, and lived their lives so far, in London. They had a mother who was a writer, no longer in her earliest youth, and a father who was an academic and teacher and the kindest man on earth.

PART ONE

Moving Out

To think up, dream up and conceive works of beauty is a delightful occupation. Like smoking magic cigars or living the life of a courtesan absorbed in her imagination. When the work appears it has all the grace of a child, the wild joy of its creation, with the scented hues of a flower and the ready juices of a fruit already tasted. This is Conception and its pleasures. A man who can draw up his plan in words is immediately thought of as extraordinary. All artists and writers have this capacity. But to bring forth and laboriously raise the child, putting it to bed full of milk each night, kissing it each morning with a mother's indefatigable love, licking it clean, endlessly clothing it in the loveliest outfits which it immediately tears; but not to be repelled by the mad upheavals of this life, and to make of them the living masterpiece that speaks through sculpture to every beholder, through literature to every intelligence, through painting to every memory, and through music to every heart: this is execution and its labours.

Balzac, La Cousine Bette

And the stone word fell
On my still-living breast.
Never mind, I was ready.
I will manage somehow.

Anna Akhmatova, 'The Sentence'

When they learn about Clara's illness, the first thing almost everyone says is: 'When did you realise? How was she diagnosed?' They want to know what the signs were.

'But if someone tells you they've got a flat tyre,' I would say, 'you don't say, "How did you know?" Aren't there other things you'd ask first, like "Can it be fixed?" Or "Do you need a lift?"' Later I came to see their curiosity more kindly. They wanted me to give them words that would keep them from evil, to stop it happening to them.

So I'd say that she didn't gain weight, however much she fed, and for the first few months I did almost nothing but feed her. Everything she took in, she threw up. At six months she kept down so little, it became pretty pointless to try to feed her at all. She caught a lung infection. She coughed. She did not thrive.

The medical professional has a way of suddenly producing a poetic word where a prosaic one would do. You almost expect the health worker who identifies a baby as 'not thriving' to lean into the crib, cackling, and ask, 'What ails thee, little mite?' But the medical and the poetic are related terms at opposite ends of a spectrum. It depends with what level of abstraction you see things. Some people see shapes in the clouds: the Virgin Mary, a ship; others see only particles, condensation, light refracted through water molecules. I look at a poem on a page and I see letters, words, but beyond that I see meaning. I knew there must be a scientific reason why my baby was so slight and sick. I had always been wary of science, having been taught early on that it wasn't for me. Now I needed to understand what the particles in her body were doing, what misprint along the chain of her DNA had caused the malfunction, what creative act of mistranslation had given rise to this state of non-thriving in a baby so very near the start of life.

She and I went back into hospital when she as a person, and I as a mother, were only a few days old, because she had lost weight since birth, even though she was feeding well – luxuriantly even, with her tiny hands dabbing at me while she sucked, and her eyes tipped back into their orbits in pleasure. But nothing showed up on 'the tests'. Week after week I took her back to be weighed. No gain. A gram here, a gram there. Then half a kilo lost. A teaching doctor mocked us in front of his students: the elderly professor and his wife. 'You just have to accept,' he said, 'you aren't producing enough milk.' I wonder, if Clara had died and a post-mortem had shown why, whether I would have drawn any comfort from saying to him, 'You just have to accept, you're a terrible doctor.'

Because she wasn't absorbing any nutrients, she became vitamin-deficient and her skin flared up. Unable to get the GP to refer us to a consultant, we paid, when she was eight months old, to see a paediatric dermatologist at a private clinic. A kind man, from South Africa, he asked me whether she tasted salty when I kissed her. He turned away to wash his hands and I tasted her. I felt a bit guilty doing it, like when you lick the spoon from the cake mixture. She tasted of mermaids, of the sea. How did you know, I asked him when he turned back. It seemed like a trick from a fairy story. 'A friend of my son's,' he said. 'He has cystic fibrosis.'

At the Royal Brompton Hospital, down the far end of the King's Road, the respiratory consultant (suddenly appointments with brilliant senior doctors on the NHS came thick and fast) held Clara and talked to her and she followed his finger with her eyes and laughed. A test showed she did have more salt on her skin than you would expect. They took blood so they could look at her DNA. There was a week to wait.

2001 wasn't a year to flirt with fear for the thrill of it. Terrible, unthinkable things actually had happened to so many people. Early on the afternoon of 11 September I was on the phone to a Microsoft helpline in Boston, waiting in a queue. 'Can you hear me, ma'am?' a woman's voice said. 'Yes,' I said. 'Hold on a second, my baby's crying.' 'Sure,' she said, in a sing-song, all-the-time-in-the world voice, a distracted voice, maybe scrolling down eBay. I put the phone down and went over to take Clara from her basket. As I came back across the room a voice on the radio said, 'We are getting unconfirmed reports . . .'

I picked up the phone again and said, 'Are you in New York?'

'No, ma'am,' she said, 'I'm in Boston right now.'

'They're saying on the radio that a plane has flown into the World Trade Center.'

'I'm not aware of that right now, ma'am. You have a good day now,' she said.

During that week of waiting I visited Waterstones in Camden High Street. I walked disdainfully past the high piles of *A Life's*

Work by Rachel Cusk. When it came to motherhood, she was on the edge of the lawn, in heels and a hat, on school sports day, while I was sweating it out on the track. Later I read it and managed to smile at her description of her newborn daughter as a 'tetchy monarch'. At the back of the shop, where they keep the scientific books and dictionaries, next to but not overlapping with the self-help books, I read an entry in a medical dictionary for cystic fibrosis. Clara was strapped to my front in a baby carrier, and I had to peer over her head to see the text. Other mothers were reading to their infants in the children's section, *Peepo!* and *Maisy Goes Camping*. I heard one mother saying to another that she just *hated* herself for letting her toddler eat an apple that wasn't organic. 'I felt like such a terrible mother!' she said. With her theatrical intonation and wide staring eyes she seemed to be making no distinction between the way she read to her child and the way she talked to her friend about the child, so that I could imagine her saying to her husband that evening in her bending-and-stretching voice, crossing her fingers behind her back: '*Down* I went to the bookshop, and *there* was a *baby*, no bigger than my *hand*!' I could feel myself inert, uninflected, not a member of any club, a free-floating particle veering towards the furthermost reaches of the set containing all good mothers, popping out of it like a little air bubble, and the cell wall sealing up behind me. As woman-with-apple dramas went, hers seemed pretty unsensational. Is the mother always to blame? I hadn't yet begun to think about the chances of my happening to make a baby with the one person in twenty-five who carries the CF gene. The chances of that baby having the illness (one in four). When did the muddle in the genetic pattern on my seventh chromosome occur? Generations back? Centuries? 'I just want my child to be happy and healthy,' I heard a woman say on the bus, quite casually, as though she was being modest in her wants, as though she wasn't asking for the moon. I covered Clara's ears, in case it was a phrase she might stock somewhere for reinspection once she had acquired some language. I suppose she meant she didn't mind how clever or beautiful or intelligent the child was. Or famous, I suppose we should add to that. Could a child suffer and be happy? Be ill and happy? Be healthy and sad? Was happiness contingent on health? Health on happiness? If health could come from happiness, could we cure her with happiness? But 'there is no known cure', the dictionary said.

Later, when I realised I had reason to fear for my daughter's life, I kept seeing my difficulties in the light of other people's losses. However ill and unhappy she was, I still had a chance to pull her clear. Now, when she is doubled up with pain at breakfast then straightens up, smiling, white, and says, 'OK now,' I think of people with Ebola, people in Gaza, Ukraine, Syria, Iraq. There are almost more of them to think of than there are happy and healthy people who need no kind of blessing.

During that week I tell the health visitor at the weigh-in that they are testing for cystic fibrosis. She looks at me in horror, and actually crosses herself. 'Please God, not that, not *that*,' she whispers hoarsely. She recovers herself. 'My neighbour's boy, he has it, you know, the cystic fibrosis. He's had a lung transplant now. Or was it his heart? One or the other! Both, maybe! He's twenty, he's . . . doing very well.' There is no mistaking, despite the recovery, that we are out of place here. This is a session for well babies. I have come through the wrong door. Her eyes, so used and worn they could be second-hand, with old pouches beneath, full of orange powder, fix on the baby. I can tell she is wishing me back out through the door.

There is a certain point after which, in any case, the GP and the health visitor are no good to you. Since reading the entry in the medical dictionary I had looked it up on the internet. I knew what it would mean. I didn't tell anyone. I was doing what my mother would have called 'keeping myself to myself'. But into my mind comes a girl who was in my class when I was maybe six years old. Her name was Annette, and she seemed to me not really like a child at all. Her hair was stiff and grey, her cheeks were sunken, she coughed all the time. There was something strange about her hands; they were dry and stiff too. The teacher asked us to join in a circle for 'Ring a Ring o' Roses' and she put her hand in mine. It was cold, like the hand of a very old person, one of my great-aunts', a hand to fumble around in a handbag with, for Polo mints and a bus pass, and I was desperate to release it long before we all fell down dead. Perhaps I did. I know she disappeared from school suddenly one day, and never returned. I think now she had cystic fibrosis, and must have died.

We returned to the hospital at the end of the week, a Friday in February. Clara was so tiny, I didn't use the pram, or even a sling. I carried her down the street from the tube station just as she was, the way you carry a dessert when you're going to have dinner with the neighbours. Nico and I were told to wait in the lobby of the hospital till someone came to fetch us. When the nurse arrived she made remarks about public transport and the weather. We rode up to the respiratory department in the lift and she showed us into the doctor's office. It must have been the end of a long week for him.

However much we like and admire the doctors who care for Clara, I always think that they are going home to robust little children who sleep through the night. I expect it is not true in all cases, by any means. I read one day about a CF doctor who had given birth to a child with CF. The gene, or genetic pattern, had been inside her all that time. And then there was the MS specialist who one day noticed a tremor in her own eyelid. There is something particularly poignant about these cases where the disease has been harboured all the time in the body, dormant, while the host person struggles to eliminate it in the outside world.

'Well,' said the kind doctor, with Winnie-the-Pooh prints on his tie, 'I'm afraid the results do show that Charlotte has cystic fibrosis.'

'Clara!' I said eagerly, leaning forward. *Tant pis* for Charlotte and her parents, in that split second. 'This is Clara.'

Glancing at his notes, he said, 'Sorry, Clara, yes. Clara has cystic fibrosis.'

There was a long silence. Clara grinned up at me. She had a tooth. Two, even. For her, nothing had changed. Several times the doctor offered us tissues, though neither of us was crying. I took one, so as not to offend.

'You'll hear us calling it CF,' he said. I suddenly felt slightly hysterical, remembering how my brother and I had giggled uncontrollably when our driving instructor, who fancied himself as Doncaster's answer to James Hunt, said, 'This is the accelerator, but you'll be hearing me call it the gas.'

He wouldn't be hearing me call it that, I thought, using a *petit nom*, a nickname, for something we would far rather not have any acquaintance with at all, let alone an intimate one. He talked about improvements in life expectancy. Some

children even survived into adulthood now, went to university. How long had these been things we couldn't take for
granted? About two minutes. Clara was eight months old.
From now on, I felt, if I let my attention falter for a second,
she would be snuffed out.

Every moment became a moment in which I protected my
baby. Some of it I did in secret, like a madwoman muttering
spells. I thought of her as a candle, cupping my hand around
her. Of course she sensed it, though I tried not to let it show.
When she was nine and we got bad news she said, 'It's OK,
Mama, you can cry. It's scary when I think you're being brave.'
We entered into a partnership that was not balanced in quite
the same way as the usual mother–daughter relationship.
She knew as much about me as I did about her. I was sure she
could see in the dark. I would wake and find her in my arms,
scrutinising me, wondering, it seemed, if I was going to be
up to this. The good news, the doctor had said, was that she
had the most common gene, twice over. Delta F508. Work
was being done on gene therapy, new treatments. There was
every possibility she could be helped.

Through these years . . . it was not my mind that grew numb, but my soul. An astonishing observation: it is precisely for feeling that one needs time, and not for thought. Thought is a flash of lightning, feeling is a ray from the most distant of stars. Feeling requires leisure; it cannot survive under fear.

Marina Tsvetaeva, quoted in Tillie Olsen, *Silences*

As long as we lived in London, Clara was looked after at Great Ormond Street. Weekly, then monthly, then later three-monthly clinics, on a Tuesday afternoon. Daily physiotherapy, antibiotics, vitamins. When they told us she would probably have to take antibiotics every day of her life, we were horrified. The doctor said, 'Well, you can try without, but within a few weeks you will be back in this office begging me to write out a prescription.' Twice a day she had to inhale vapour from a noisy machine that ran for twenty minutes. It was called a nebuliser, but we called it the Green Machine. She might as well start learning her colours.

Nico paced the floor with her at night as she cried – *I'm hungry, I'm hungry, I've fed all day and all night, and my mother's sleeping, and I'm still hungry!* – reciting poems he'd invented on his walks to and from Bloomsbury, through Regent's Park, about elephants in the zoo and the wakeful baby; he changed her nappies while talking to her gently but in a tone that suggested – and promised, faithfully – a whole interesting world of things he could introduce her to and explain, one day, not the least interesting of which was the way she could tip up on her minute bottom and put her doll-size legs up in the air towards the ceiling, just so. His tone has not really altered, all these years later. When they stand in front of a painting in the National Gallery, side by side, and he talks to her about the composition, or the story, or the brushwork, and her eyes flick from the canvas to her father and back, he uses a tone that implies that he is as fascinated by this as anyone hearing it for the first time might be, that he doesn't own the knowledge, but is, like her, newly in receipt of it.

Right from the start, people asked me: 'Are you writing?' I'd always written, and until the birth of Clara I had written for a living. But it was my psychic, not economic well-being people were concerned about – a misplaced concern, I felt, which betrayed a failure on their part to understand both the priorities of any new mother and the extremity of our situation. It also added another layer of guilt. I hadn't 'gone back to work', even if I was both exhausted and fulfilled by the unstinting labour of caring for my beloved child. It was like being nagged to get back out on the game, to prove your employability and your right to work, when you were actually choosing to stay at home in bed with the one you loved. My diaries for that time in my life are all empty. My mental health must have been poor but life was vivid, and imbued into every last crack and crevice with love. I felt I was doing the work I loved, with and for my child. It was fear, checked somewhere inside me, almost never expressed, that stopped me writing, not unhappiness. I felt I needed to contain everything within me, that to write, even if I had time or been able, would have been to squander a kind of power – *force* in French (feminine) – which was needed for tending and nurturing, and if possible healing. A French psychoanalyst friend seemed to believe writing, for women in particular, had magical powers, that I could somehow write her well, if I wanted.

Instead I played the piano, a solitary, face-to-the-wall occupation. I learned the Chopin G minor ballade, which was intricate, soaring, angry, devastated music. It wasn't the emotional outlet that helped, though, it was the fiendish nature of the fingering, the impossible jumps and stretches, the crashing chords and tripping cadenzas – it was a physical release, like throwing yourself around in a padded cell, bouncing off walls.

At first I had felt unable to draw a line between cystic fibrosis and anything else I knew. Then I read an article claiming that Chopin had died not of tuberculosis, as had always been thought, but of cystic fibrosis. The Poles, who had his heart while the rest of him lay in Paris, refused for many years to allow it to be disinterred for testing. Like many amateur pianists I had felt close to Chopin for years, in that odd way you can feel close to composers, or writers or artists, daily absorbing their most intimate feelings intravenously into your own life's blood. I have read a number of discouraging articles about Chopin, what a difficult man he was, snobbish and querulous, but I like to think that if, for a while, George Sand loved him, he can't have been all bad. Nico worked fifteen-hour days, getting up at six with Clara, sitting her in the little screw-on seat at the island table in the kitchen, sponging splashes off his beautiful shirts; or talking to her companionably, standing at the window of our first-floor flat with her in his arms, showing her the cherry blossom and lilac. I dreaded the sound of the door closing behind him as he left to go to work.

It would be nice to think, in life, that you could be judged a little by the quality of the people who love you.

The cystic fibrosis gene had unfolded itself in our daughter's body like a paper flower meeting water. Now I could think of it as Chopin's gene. Inhabiting Chopin at the piano, or being inhabited by him, whichever way around it was, I was also embracing the gene, accepting it. A gene isn't a 'thing', though, much as I liked to think of it as such, as though I'd been bequeathed a locket of Chopin's, or a ring. It's a sequence, a pattern of proteins, just as a sentence is a string of words, a pattern of letters. It takes only one typo, one letter in the wrong place, to change the pattern. The interpretation of the message by the protein-making mechanism leads to the development of the disease, with its various devastating symptoms. An American scientist, noting the similarity between chains of proteins making up a gene that finds expression in a particular condition (having blue eyes, having problems shifting salt molecules) and musical notes that form clusters and melodies, had invented a system for translating protein sequences into music. You can imagine the results might sound similar to certain experimental works by contemporary composers. Some of them do. But some of them sound more like things we are already familiar with. The author had back-translated a Chopin nocturne (opus 55 no. 1) into a DNA sequence which turned out to bear a quite remarkable similarity to a genetic pattern they might have expected to find had they been granted permission to disinter Chopin's heart and analyse the protein sequences. Reading this made me feel rather queasy. It sounded more like Scientology than science, something disreputable and self-referential. But I was glad, at least, to discover Clara was a member of a set that may have included Chopin.

Chopin's heart was finally exhumed on the night of 14 April 2014, in the presence of thirteen people, scientists and 'other experts' − musicians, perhaps − together with the Archbishop of Warsaw. The jar of cognac containing the precious organ, repatriated from Paris to Warsaw after his burial at Père Lachaise, was disinterred, inspected, photographed, prayed over, then returned to its resting place. A forensic scientist remarked, 'The spirit of this night was most sublime.' All those present were sworn to secrecy. Nothing has been published. No genetic analysis took place, so far as is known. It remains unclear whether he died of cystic fibrosis. People generally prefer the diagnosis of TB. Tuberculosis chic looked a lot like heroin chic, and must have given a leg-up to many a lesser artistic talent than Chopin's. Whatever he died of, it remains a mystery – to some, though not to me – how someone so unwell for so much of his life could have produced music of such extraordinary beauty. In the end, the poetic interest was placed above the scientific one. The Polish Culture Minister remarked, 'We in Poland often say Chopin died longing for his homeland. Additional information which could be gained about his death would not be sufficient reason to disturb Chopin's heart.'

A week after Clara was born, and a few days before she was readmitted to hospital, my parents drove down the A1, stopped as always at Sainsbury's in Bedfordshire for a bun and a cup of tea and, after the usual frantic flurry with parking vouchers, rang the bell at the flat. I'd begun to notice that every time my mother came through a door she stumbled through it as though she'd been out wandering all night on a blasted heath. I remember looking at her and thinking, Something's very wrong. She sat on the sofa in her coat with the baby on her knee, not moving, just being with her, as though infusing her with something, for a long time. My father, on the other hand, threw her and nuzzled her, pressed her nose like a little button for summoning a lift, and sang to her. He watched over her when she slept, and when she was diagnosed he adopted a tone of vigorous optimism, which he preserves to this day.

When Clara was a few months old my mother offered to take the baby for a walk in the pram. 'I loved walking you when you were little.' 'What if she gets hungry?' 'We'll come home again, won't we, darling?' she said happily, peering in at Clara, on to whose tiny features I was already projecting my own mistrust. They left the house, and I fell into a deep sleep. I dreamed I had a review to write, an imminent deadline, and hadn't even read the book, which in the dream was *The Tiger Who Came to Tea* and was very long and dense, with pages of footnotes. I would need to read the secondary literature in the British Library. Did I have time to get there and back before they returned? At once my eyes jerked open and the flat was empty. Where was my mother? Where was my baby? I checked the clock. They'd been gone two and a half hours. Clara was so hungry; I didn't yet know why, but she needed to feed constantly. Had I been quite mad to let them out of my sight? I was guilty – of sleeping. I ran out into the street. No sign. I ran around the web of roads nearby, past the church, the library, up to the park, back again, to the doctor's surgery, anywhere I could think of. I got home. My mother was outside, sitting on the step, rocking the pram. 'Hello, dear. Did you get lost?'

'*I* didn't, no. Did you?'

'Oh no. But we went all round the houses. And past the ship.'

'Ship?' We were miles from the river.

'The blue and white liner. In the dock.'

She must have meant the block of flats on the main road, which had recently been painted blue and white. We went back into the flat and I fed Clara and sat down to write my review. The book's title in French had been *Mal de Mer*, a pun equating seasickness and motherhood. The English translator had given it the title *Breathing Underwater*. My father returned from his shopping trip in Oxford Street with a pair of competitively priced trousers from Marks & Spencer. Nico was in Italy. 'Here's Daddy,' my mother told Clara. 'There's something wrong,' I told him later. 'She's losing her—' But what was she losing? Her grip? Her mind? Her faculties? Her senses? Her sense of direction?

When Clara was diagnosed I told my parents straight away. I phoned them with the news almost a year to the day after I had told them I was expecting a baby. But I don't think my mother ever took it in. In a drawer by her bed, after she died, I found several notes in her handwriting, on scraps of paper. The letters were more spaced out than they had been when she was young and well and busy; you could read the effort of spelling, of word composition, where before words had just been discrete blocks of cursive script with a meaning. *New milk first by thumb when open fridge door*, read one. Even I found that quite complicated, but I knew my father must have told her she should use up the least fresh milk first. What a complicated idea that must have been for her – opening the fridge door, for a start. Which way does it open? Left side? Right side? Like a book? Milk in the door. Bottom shelf. My thumb – here, this one. New milk. Not good. Take old milk – good. Not near my thumb. There. Away from thumb. It makes me feel giddy, again, to think of it. Another note says, *Memory clinic – oh how I wish we had not started down this road. Frightened.* And a diary entry. *Cistic fibers.* Crossed out. Try again. *Sisters fibrosis.*

The English are a literary people, they prefer the idea of a thing to the thing itself.

Virginia Woolf, *The Diary of Virginia Woolf*

When my cousin decided to move to France – perhaps there's a gene for it – her children's nanny came to work for us. I was a bit apprehensive, as nannying was something I had done for other people and not something I'd ever imagined anyone would do for me. The first morning, I went out into Camden, with Clara in the pushchair, to meet Bobbie, and saw her coming towards us down Parkway from the tube with a bunch of daffodils in her fist. I held my hand out to receive them. 'Actually,' she said, moving them out of my reach, 'they're not for you. They're for Clara.' I had become so used to people commiserating with me I had forgotten that flowers could be for celebration, an expression of delight.

Bobbie set us on our feet, and made me laugh. We got on our knees together and scrubbed the stained carpets, we pored over prescriptions and instructions for use, and she carried Clara on her shoulders as she grew. In all these years, she is the only person outside the immediate family who ever learned what medicines Clara needed and how to administer them. By the time she left to have her own late, miraculous baby, I was immeasurably stronger, less afraid.

When Clara was almost three, our second daughter was born. If there was a French reflexive verb for giving birth to yourself, that would be the one to use for what Verity did in the Elizabeth Garrett Anderson Hospital. As much as everything around Clara was medicalised and monitored and scrutinised, so everything to do with Verity seemed to happen while someone was sneezing, or looking the other way. We had been in the hospital two or three minutes, and were put in a waiting room. The midwife went out into the corridor to look for the paperwork. She came back in and found us sitting on the floor with a newborn baby where two minutes earlier there hadn't been one. She clearly thought we had pinched her off the ward. It was such a joy, to produce a baby like that, into her father's hands, a baby we already knew didn't have CF. With her arrival everything steadied up and stabilised.

We decided we'd move to France as soon as Nico retired. He didn't want to turn into one of those faculty ghosts who haunt the library stacks. It seemed a lovely idea. The children would go to the village school, and one day to *lycée*. I had lived much of my adult life in France, having been somehow set up to love it from an early age. Love it? To look for it, maybe. I inherited the idea of France from my parents. All through my childhood, 'Ah, France' was said on a sigh, a downward hushing tone, already a place remembered, lost, regretted. That was its charm. It was the lost domain before I ever found it.

My father had studied in Montpellier for a year when he was at Birmingham University. Photos survive of a very young man in shirtsleeves, already in training to be a Methodist local preacher, posing with a baguette, about to hop on a bus to Nîmes for the weekly Protestant temple service, 1950. There was a poetry to France, the idea of France, which I detected in my parents' voices when they spoke of the first holiday they spent together, on the Ile Saint-Louis. The phrase, this inscrutable series of sounds, was like a word in itself, meaning 'longing'. In 1974 we actually visited France, and I made my first acquaintance with what I thought of as

England's closet cousin, who dressed, ate, smelled, danced, spoke quite differently, and was only visible at certain times of the year. We flew to Le Bourget in a plane from East Midlands Airport and stayed in a hotel just behind the Moulin Rouge. The lift between floors was a green-painted cage. My parents taught me to say, '*Encore du sucre, s'il vous plaît, madame,*' and sent me into the kitchen with a bowl. In the evenings we ate chicken and chips and chocolate ice cream. There were *filles de joie* in every doorway in our street. My father suggested they were 'shop girls' waiting for buses.

Every day we went out visiting. We slogged round the Louvre; or up the Eiffel Tower; or to Fontainebleau, where we were reproached by a *garde nationale* for eating our home-made sandwiches on a bench opposite Napoleon's bedroom; or to Versailles, where I desperately hoped we might repeat the experience of Miss Moberly and Miss Jourdain, who stepped back into the time of Marie Antoinette when visiting the gardens in 1901. We went to the Galeries Lafayette and looked up at the painted ceiling, and my father bought us notebooks with squared paper.

When I was around fifteen, my piano teacher gave me a book: *Le Grand Meaulnes*. I struggled through it, and the dimness of my understanding of it in a way supplemented my reading, since it was a book about scarcely apprehended things, places glimpsed in the mist, people half forgotten, encountered perhaps in a dream. Alain-Fournier, the author, had died in the First World War. I had never seen a dead body, though I had had vivid, very visual dreams about war as a small child, mostly about waiting, sitting under trees waiting, cleaning equipment and waiting. I don't know where these images could have come from as at that stage we didn't have a television and never went to the cinema. No one I knew had ever died, only people in history books and songs. I imagined Rupert Brooke, and Alain-Fournier after him, found in the river with his toes turned up, after weeks spent lolling in the corner of a foreign field, boots crossed at the ankles, chewing on a stalk of grass. This misconceived image of the events of the Great War probably owed something to the complete absence of images for it in my childhood. There were no films, photos or paintings in our lives that might have supplied illustration. Uncle Eddie, who lived on a very steep hill in Sheffield, smoked an acrid pipe and had a small brass turtle with threepenny bits in on the mantelpiece, had been in it. He was said 'never to speak' about it, and spent most of his time making dolls' houses. My maternal grandfather had run away to fight at the front at fourteen, and been sent home only on being discovered still to be underage a year later. They were all old men, so that it seemed to have been a war for old men, and the children of my generation, the grandchildren of the combatants, felt that it was a war that all the old men had survived; only young men had been killed. These ruptured literary lives had a poignant appeal to me as a morbidly literary teenager. What I connected with was the young men's idyll, which was closely bound to their doomed awakening sexuality and awareness of the fleeting nature of childhood.

And just as we were encouraged to believe that 'Jesus died for me', I believed that certain writers who died before I was born had written their books for me. Nico told me about a don in Oxford who regularly stole medieval books from a library in the belief that he, who knew so much more about them, who loved them more than anyone, was their rightful inheritor. Aged fourteen, had I had access, I could have lifted the manuscript of 'If I should die . . . ' from the Bodleian without a qualm. The poem itself was *about* appropriation. France is that foreign field whose very charm is to have a corner that's for ever England. Not because we want there to be a Tesco on the outskirts of Poitiers where they sell Marmite or digestive biscuits, but because in that rich earth is interred our *longing* for France, which is hopelessly English.

Next to the closet-cousin image of France I had formed as a child and young woman, I carried a more realistic idea, its non-identical twin, from which most of the clichés had been extracted. There were no castles in this second image, no *boulangeries* with bicycles propped outside them, no markets or rows of vines, not a single café nor even a house of honey-coloured stone set back from a road with plane trees planted on either side. There was a river, though, for some reason, and a small boat tethered to an iron post in the reeds. I thought it was drawn from a short story by Maupassant, *'Une Partie de Campagne'* perhaps, and that Corot was the painter who had chosen this aspect of France to paint, but when I re-read *'Une Partie de Campagne'* it didn't correspond, and nor did the paintings of Corot; though they were closer, lacking the Maupassantian elements of suspense and spite.

We began house-hunting in the west of France, inland from Bordeaux, but some canny estate agents showed us a photograph of a flat-fronted house with a grey door in a different *département* altogether. George Sand's house at Nohant, north of Brive, where she and Chopin by some accounts spent some happy summers, has been described as a *'maison souriante'*, and my first impression was that this house too was smiling, that it beamed serenely from the photograph.

We decided to go and look, even though it was in the wrong place.

We came from the north over the Causses, the high, limestone heathland that is deeply fissured by the great river valleys of central France. The major rivers are sometimes red with strong iron deposits from upstream after rain, but the lesser courses on this higher ground often run chalky white or even blue. It is difficult to describe in a few words. Now I am living in Somerset, I can feel the shape of the landscape I have left behind in France, as someone might feel the absence of a long-loved partner in the bed they have shared for many years. Sometimes the smells were resinous and Mediterranean, though there were none of the same trees, and little *garrigue*. But the stones were white as Provençal stones and the animals were pretty in the fields, and a line of trees could make you stop still on the road as you walked, and draw your eyes up to the hills. It was warm and ancient and full of rivers and trees and old houses and farms. For seven years it was our home.

It was too short a time. I had always thought we would stay there for ever. Our children would grow up half French and half English, and would probably move to England to discover that the world they grew up half knowing, from books and from their parents' friends who came visiting with their children, was not quite what they had been led to believe, but for the time being was more interesting and diverse. A cure would be found for cystic fibrosis. Perhaps one of them, or both, would bring their children there, and sit out at the table in the courtyard off the kitchen and gossip and plan while they prepared the evening meal. (I hesitate to say top and tail beans, or even hull strawberries or slice up apples, because I want to avoid that way of writing about France. When I wrote a book about France once before and the publishers gave it a cover with a *boulangerie* and a bicycle I was mortified. It was someone else's idea of the thing, far from the thing itself.)

As she stood there, half dreaming in the water a few feet from the shore, the strange feeling crept over her that this had all happened before. It would have been difficult to explain what she meant by this, but it was almost as though she were now standing outside of herself, somewhere farther back, watching herself standing there in the water – a small figure in her best blue dress with her socks and shoes in her hand, looking across the staithe at the old house with many windows.

Joan G. Robinson, *When Marnie Was There*

When we visited the house it was raining.

My heart sank as we entered the building. Oh dear, I thought, we are going to buy this beautiful house. It corresponded so perfectly to the kind of house I had come across in books as a child, reading with my back to the radiator in my bedroom in a newly built house on a housing estate in South Yorkshire. It was ample, solid, older than its inhabitants by many centuries, with land around which could be unscrambled to reveal the designs and schemes of long-dead gardeners. But I could not imagine what we would do here. Eventually the removal van arrived with all our books, many thousands of them, and even opening the grey front door I was reminded of the hand gesture you'd use to open a book.

Clara came home from school one day when she was about nine and, excited, showed me a story in her French textbook. It was by André Maurois, and the title was 'La Maison'. The narrator, a woman, says that several years before, during an illness, she repeatedly dreamed the same dream, in which, while walking in the country, she saw a white house, and was drawn towards it. On one occasion she even approached the house and rang the bell, but no one answered.

After recovering from her illness, she decides to look for the house. She is convinced it must exist, and that she must have known it as a child, but has no memory of it other than in the dream. Soon she becomes obsessed by the need to find the house, and spends a summer driving round France, looking for it. But '*Je ne vous raconterai pas mes voyages,*' she says. I won't tell you about my travels.

The woman eventually finds the house, rings the bell. The man who opens the door apologises: the owners are absent, and he is only there to show round a prospective tenant. The owners have left the house because it's haunted. The woman laughs.

'You of all people should know better than to laugh,' says the man. 'For the ghost was you!'

I tried to get Clara to explain what it was about the story that drew her so, but she didn't know. It wasn't that she had felt she had known our house before, more that she had known this story before. She went back to school the next day and asked the teacher where the story came from. Where was the rest of it? 'That's it,' the teacher said. 'There is no more.' There was no longer novel from which it was extracted, which she could discover, enter and explore. And I too would have wished it otherwise. 'One summer, having learned to drive a small car . . . ': I liked that sentence. What things my mother would have done with it! And: '*Je ne vous raconterai pas mes voyages.*' What a heavenly unopened parcel that was! Though I would have preferred it if the French for ghost had been *revenant*, rather than *fantôme*. 'Do you think the woman rented the house?' Clara wanted to know. 'Was she the tenant the man was waiting for? How did he know she would come, when she didn't know herself? Why did she have the dream when she was ill? Did she actually die? Is she dead now? Is finding the house just a dream?'

What if, she said, the man writing the story just dreamed it?

~

All the houses in the old port or *faubourg* were fifteenth-century or earlier in origin. Ours had once been three small houses, which were joined together and squared up by a lawyer, a *notaire*, at the beginning of the nineteenth century, perhaps when Napoleon was Consul, or away on campaigns. I imagined the man who put our house together as a figure from Balzac, later awarded some civic distinction that blazed on his frock coat.*

During the day, light poured on to the first floor like liquid amber. The wood gleamed and glowed. But at night, when I moved about, unable to sleep, listening for Clara's cough, the floors, walls, doorways and paintings were all grey, black, a tarnished silver colour, and I had the impression of sliding rectangles, moving in and over and away from each other, a series of empty frames with empty rooms beyond, even though I knew the books were there, and the coloured toys and the clothes and letters and everything that indicated human habitation. It was as though I had intimations of the house emptying before it ever did. Animals do the same thing as us, making homes that may be used by successive owners, over generations, but they don't have the problem of contents. When I was a child, at Lytham St Annes, the beach was

---

* 'You see a short, fat man, in good health, dressed all in black, self-assured, almost always stiff, pedantic, above all self-important! His outer mask, bloated with an unctuous stupidity which was at first feigned but has over time become interiorised, now suggests the inscrutability of a diplomat, but without his subtlety — and I shall tell you why. You are struck, in particular, by that butter-coloured pate, which speaks of hours of toil, boredom, inner arguments, the turmoil of youth and the absence of all passion. You say to yourself: this gentleman looks extraordinarily like a lawyer.' (Honoré de Balzac, *Le Notaire*)

covered in the casts of sandworms, discarded houses – though I didn't know that, and always associated them with spaghetti hoops. How long did those creatures live for, inhabiting their houses? Were they actually not houses but birth cases of some kind, the shells in which they grew to maturity?

There was a number of portraits in the house, so that sometimes it seemed to be populated by more people than actually lived in it, and when we moved out, until the house was emptied they occupied it in our absence. On my desk was my favourite picture of Nico, a black and white photograph. His head is turned away to the right, he is animated, as though following the flight path of a bird or of one of his own quick, winged thoughts. Recently a friend made a drawing of him in pencil. Again he is looking to the right, but this time it is as though he is receding slowly, like someone with his back to the engine in a train, watching the landscape slip away.

Clara Schumann was in the playroom – just a poster from an exhibition about female composers held in Vienna, showing a pen-and-ink drawing of her in 1836, aged seventeen. She has a high forehead, an unfashionably shaped nose, large oval eyes and a slender neck, and is an unmistakable beauty. She had been secretly corresponding with Robert for some months, though they had been forcibly separated by her over-zealous father, and was about to embark on an exhausting series of concert tours. Her life as a composer came to an end with Robert's death, though she continued with her hugely successful career as a performer. She was the mother of eight children too. But in 1839 she wrote in her diary, 'I once thought that I possessed creative talent, but I have given up this idea; a woman must not desire to compose – not one has been able to do it, and why should I expect to? It would be arrogance.' Everyone who has ever tried to create something, to bring into existence what previously was inexistent, has written similar things in their diary, I imagine. I like to think it was only a temporary moment of despair. Indeed, she did not stop composing at that point and a few years later she wrote: 'There is no greater joy than composing music oneself and listening to it.' I keep her picture on the wall for myself and my daughters.

On the upstairs landing hung a portrait known in Nico's family as 'the ancestress' – a late-eighteenth-century picture of a little girl of about eight, in a flouncy dress and ringlets, her hand touching the branch of a tree that fills the upper right-hand side of the picture. A robin sits in the branch, and her little tipped foot is tentatively feeling for the bottom of the picture frame. In Nico's study was a photo of our children, standing with their backs to the portrait of the ancestress, holding a photo of Nico and his sister taken in front of the ancestress when they were small. This technique of featuring the work of art in the work of art – of a not very grand type, in these instances – is called *mise-en-abîme*, 'placed into the abyss'.

In the photo of our children what I find most interesting is not the repetition of the painting, which appears twice, or of the three generations – the ancestress, their father and aunt, and Clara and Verity – or even the three different media: oil paint, black and white photography, and digital colour. I enjoy the very 1950s character of the black and white photograph of Nico and Sasha: Nico's grey flannel shirt, the intelligence in his face, the expression that is so familiar to me captured by the camera long before I was born; Sasha's resemblance to Verity at the same age, but with dark hair, in a style Verity had for a while, cut by Nico. What really hooks me, in fact, is

35

the new information incorporated each time, the deviation. Because we have the original portrait of the ancestress on the wall, perhaps with the CF gene sitting somewhere inside her – though obviously we don't have the girl herself, or her robin or the branch – all the later images suggest a progression, a coming forward in time and an accumulation, unlike most instances of the *mise-en-abîme*, which seem to suggest a fullness, reducing through regression.

When I look at the portrait of the ancestress, it is remarkable to think that she could have the gene too. Through all those generations the gene from Nico's side was waiting to be put with its other half and make a baby who would have the disease. There was a cartoon on TV when I was a child called *Shazzan*. In a mysterious chest, two children find two halves of a ring; when the halves are put together the word 'Shazzan' is formed. When the children say the word, they are magically transported to the story-within-a-story world of the Arabian Nights, where they meet a genie called Shazzan who presents them, by the by, with a magic flying camel. Clara got the two halves of the ring together – there is only a one-in-four chance with each pregnancy, when both parents are carriers, that this will happen – but there were no flying camels. People kept telling us to hope, though.

A friend of my sister-in-law, who worked for the Cystic Fibrosis Trust, looked me squarely in the eye one day when Clara was still a baby, and I was just beginning to realise what the future held, and said, 'She's going to be OK.' There wasn't much reason to believe her, but I did. Like so many others, I have learned the power of magical thinking.

~

36

I keep the pens and pencils on my desk in a tin that once held chocolate powder, made by a Dutch company called Droste. The picture on the tin shows a nurse in a starched headdress carrying, on a tray, a cup of cocoa and a tin of cocoa powder. On the tin on her tray can be seen another, smaller replica of the tin bearing the image of the nurse and her tray, which itself displays a smaller replica still, and so on. The possibilities for infinite recession are limited only by the diminishing size of the multiple nesting images, which eventually become invisible to the eye, and irreproducible by any printing process. As we peer in to get a close look at the furthermost image we seem to topple headlong in time and space, into an abyss.

Mise-en-abîme is a widely used – some might say overused – visual and literary device. During the writing this book was called *Mise en Abîme*, but people don't much like works with foreign titles, barring *Bonjour Tristesse* and *Kama Sutra*, and I can see it isn't very catchy; though said quickly – *meezen-abim!* – it has an attractive North African tang.

The idea itself, on the other hand, *is* quite catchy. Once you start peering into mirrors, translating translations, telling stories of stories that told stories, it becomes difficult to conceive of the world in any other way. The entire universe, and the existence of every particle in it, begins to seem explicable only in terms of a giant *mise-en-abîme*. Perhaps I was attracted, too, by the 'e' on the end of *mis*, that feminine ending. The very sound of the phrase as a whole, the repeated 'ee', suggests a woman being flung off her feet and hurled *en abîme*, into the abyss.

Mise-en-abîme is a term taken from heraldry – on a crest or shield it is common to find a miniature version of the crest itself inserted into the design, and at the heart of the inserted image a smaller replica still, ad infinitum. Medieval instances of *mise-en-abîme* abound. In the Stefaneschi triptych, painted for the original St Peter's in Rome, Giotto depicts himself in a detail of the painting presenting the triptych to the Pope, rather as Hitchcock features in his own films, enjoying the double delight of being both subject and object, observer and observed. Perhaps it is this duality that appeals, tempting us with the idea that we might be both author and character, monarch and subject, lover and beloved, creator and created, the red side of the apple and the green. In a way it is an anarchic gesture, rejecting the anterior power, explaining genesis and revealing the trick behind the magic. At the same time, though, the infinite replication and recursion hooks us and pulls the thread all the way back to Genesis, or Plato, to the idea of some ideal of which everything else is only an image. 'I've forgotten more than you'll ever know,' my Scottish grandmother used to say to me in my uppity teens. This was related, in my mind, to my mother's wistful quotation of 'Intimations of Immortality'. That we are the fading lights of a distant, brighter star.

Maybe, though, if an image itself can be the begetter as well as the begotten, we can step away from despair over our littleness, our being only a pale imitation, and assume some existential command. Are we going forwards or relating backwards? Are we laying the trail of white pebbles or tracing it home, falling backwards into the abyss, or tumbling forwards into time and space? I can never be sure. Some people, though not that many, believe in human perfectibility. Genetic modification, cures for all ills, better water, diets, global understanding – perhaps all these things could lead us to some sort of heaven. Most people take a more Platonic view, in which the Chinese Whisper transmits and sometimes wilfully corrupts the original, in an extended version of the story of the Fall, beginning with the Tree of Life and ending up with deforestation and a scarred, uninhabitable, unsustainable world. Chinese Whispers being more interesting in the long run than Chinese boxes, though I have always disliked the game and the way people deliberately introduce misunderstanding to make it funnier or more interesting. Po-faced, as a child I always made a point of trying to get the message to loop back unchanged – not a popular strategy.

When I was pregnant with Verity they took a sample of the placenta, using a needle through my abdomen, and tested for CF. We waited a week for the results. When finally the phone call came, I was talking on my mobile to a friend who had called from America. I answered the home phone and my friend overheard me talking to the doctor at UCH, exclaiming with relief at the good news that the baby would be OK, crying with happiness. I felt foolish, afterwards, that I had not had the presence of mind to say, 'I have to take this, I'll call you back.' But she was by now crying too, in America, peering in from the rim of our little aural *mise-en-abîme*.

Almost all photographic examples of visual *mise-en-abîmes* seem disappointing; often even rather awful. It may be because whenever people get overexcited by a concept, poetry goes out of the window. Escher's drawings intrigue us when we are adolescents. But I don't find them powerful or beautiful, I find them sterile, without flavour. Flavour comes from distortion, misrepresentation. It develops out of craft and hand-madeness, a process that allows for interpolations, mistakes, defects, or a game with mirrors, where the light may fail or distort. The mistakes, though, have to be genuine, otherwise it's too much like one of those pirate maps you dunk in tea and age in the oven on a baking tray. In *The Arnolfini Portrait* Van Eyck has actually used a mirror behind the couple, in which they are reflected, but only once, and what I like about that painting is that everyone's attention goes first to the woman's apparent pregnancy and not to the *mise-en-abîme*.

The easiest way to create an instant *mise-en-abîme* is to place two mirrors in front of each other to produce an infinitely receding corridor. In his book *I Am a Strange Loop* the American neuroscientist Douglas Hofstadter tells how he went with his parents to buy a video camera when he was a child. This was in the very early days of video cameras, and you bought the camera along with the screen on which the images you filmed would appear. Hofstadter, in a spirit of curiosity, was about to turn the camera on the screen itself when the salesman intervened, warning him that it would break the machine if he did this. Of course this was completely untrue: he had confused breaking a taboo with breaking a machine (in stories this often happens). When Hofstadter did eventually conduct the experiment he found that the constant looping between camera and screen, as the camera picked up and then transmitted the image of itself, on and on, over and over, created a fascinating corridor. And that if you allowed the camera to pick up a bit of the edge of the screen, the rogue external element would introduce into the experiment all sorts of fascinating variations and fertile images. Hofstadter takes this looping a step further when he considers consciousness in the same light: 'The depth and complexity of human memory is staggeringly rich. Little wonder, then, that when a human being, possessed of such a rich armamentarium of concepts and memories with which to work, turns its attention to itself, as it inevitably must, it produces a self-model that is extraordinarily rich and tangled. That deep and tangled self-model is what "I"-ness is all about.'

Long after I read his book on consciousness and the folding, mutating, replicating, misshaping events that form it, I discovered that Douglas Hofstadter was also interested in translation, which he calls '[using] my own native language – and, more specifically, my own deeply personal style of crafting, manipulating, and savouring phrases in my native language – to rewrite someone else's book'. His own method of translating *La Chamade* by Françoise Sagan (his title: *That Mad Ache*) was first to transcribe a whole paragraph in French, then to translate it into English, just as, he says, 'the transcription of a strand of DNA results in a strand of RNA, and it is soon followed by the translation of that very strand of RNA into one or more proteins (via the genetic code). This two-stage process lies at the heart of all life on earth.'

Once, Hofstadter conducted an experiment in which he gave a copy of a poem by Clément Marot, a Renaissance poet, to something like sixty friends, most of them writers, and collated their translations into a book called *Le Ton Beau de Marot*. The poem was written in the autumn of 1537, as a get-well note for Jeanne d'Albret, daughter of Marguerite de Navarre. One of the translations was by a professor of neurolinguistics who spent summers in our village. We must have been one of the few households in the world to own a copy of *Le Ton Beau de Marot* – someone had given it to Nico. When the professor came to tea he was so excited to see it on our bookshelf that his teacup rattled in its saucer and the tea splashed over the sides. This strange looping connection back to the man who had first described the rich and tangled meezen-abîmey web that goes to make up selfhood was so serendipitously pleasing, I began to think it was probably a form of paranoia on my part, unconsciously choosing to see only the connections that fed my need to feel that there were 'more things in heaven and earth', etc. As my mother would have said.

The clock's 'tick-tock' I take to be a model of what we call a plot, an organisation which humanises time by giving it a form; and the interval between 'tock' and 'tick' represents purely successive, disorganised time of the sort we need to humanise.

Frank Kermode, *The Sense of an Ending*

Nico liked the fact that the only reference to the French Revolution affecting the village that he could discover was in a local history book, which mentions that in 1789, on the occasion of a small earthquake, the church clock stopped. For a short while there was no recorded time. We had a neighbour who was due to go to Colombia for two years to record the disappearing language of an Amazonian people. She came to dinner, and took home a helping of dessert for her lodger. We said our farewells and vowed we would all meet again in two years' time. The next day Clara was unwell and was sleeping in our bed in the afternoon. She was woken by the sound of the bell down below. I half opened the shutter. Elsa had brought the dish back. 'Who is it?' Clara asked from the bed. 'Just Elsa.' She sat bolt upright, eyes wide: 'Elsa? I've been asleep for two years?' And some time later Verity slept for almost a whole day when she had a fever, and opened her eyes in the early evening and said, 'I think I fell asleep for a minute!'

The long present tense that presides in this kind of instance is the only tense in which it is possible to step aside from time. In some ways that is, to me, what the experience of making music offers. Although music occurs in time, and time and rhythm are its casement, that time often seems to pass differently from ordinary time. It is more like dream time, in which seconds need to be measured in volts, or

44

some unit of power, rather than in units of length. It presides over childhood too, during which no structuring or editing eye, not even memory's lazy eye, intervenes.

When I was a child we were not well-off, and music lessons were expensive. Nor did my parents have a strong interest in music, though everyone sang, all the time – in the car, in the house, at church – and my father, who claimed to know nothing about music, automatically improvised a tenor line to all the hymns. My mother had had piano lessons, which must have been an enormous financial stretch for her parents: my grandfather worked on the mail ships that sailed from Liverpool to the west coast of Africa and back, and they lived in a council house on an estate which was heavily bombed during the war. They used the piano to form one side of the air-raid shelter in the living room. My mother said they chose to stay in the house in their own shelter rather than go to the Anderson. It was typical of my mother's family, to have chosen the cloistered but insecure cover of the piano to the collective get-togethers in the street. It was always understood that my grandmother's standoffishness, as it was called, was due to her being 'from Aberdeen'. She didn't mix. My mother's piano lessons continued through the war. She went to a man who, once she reached adolescence, showed her postcards of ladies with no clothes on. 'Didn't you think that was really strange?' I said. She had no sense of what we would understand as 'abuse' or even, really, of 'inappropriate behaviour', though if couples kissed in public spaces in the 1970s while we were having a family picnic, one of my parents would go over and order them to desist. My brother and I learned to feel hot-cheeked shame, not at promiscuity but at prudishness.

'No-o,' she said, considering the idea. 'I just thought they looked rather cold.'

When, having tried my godmother's piano, I asked whether I could have lessons, my mother bought a thin-sounding but decent modern upright, and 'went out to work' to pay for lessons. She took a part-time job in what she called a 'potty little prep school'. But I was lucky, I know, that my parents said yes when I asked to be allowed to learn. That's all it comes down to, really. That's where the luxury comes in. They knew that if a child ardently wishes to play an instrument or sing it is a good thing to help them do it. If I try to think of my childhood without music, it is full of holes, and the experience of learning instruments and singing has had a more profound influence on the shape of my adult life than anything else.

My fascination with the organ originated with Sunday-morning services when I was a child, when the local solicitor played in church and I heard Bach for the first time. It was the central Methodist church in Doncaster, built in 1832 (repeal of the Corn Laws, my mother would say, glancing up at the date on the façade as we passed inside in our Sunday best to be handed our burgundy-bound hymnbooks) on a classical design, with a gallery and high pews with brass fastenings and a shelf in front to put your hymnbook on. The plaster on the walls was painted in pale pinks and baby blues, like in a nursery. The pulpit was a vast ship, at the prow of which stood the black-surpliced figure with white X flaps on his chest, the minister – who had lately risen from his bed with his wife, and stood before the shaving mirror. His children – his own and those he had adopted, from Ghana, Nigeria, Gabon – were no holier than anyone else's and also tried to skip Sunday School by hiding in the passage with their backs up to the shiny brick wall, flattening themselves when the superintendent came looking for defectors. One year he rode on a horse around the three shires, Nottinghamshire, Lincolnshire and Yorkshire, stopping to preach at market crosses and under beech trees, like John Wesley.

The choir huddled, pre-service, in a little room on the first floor, carpeted and panelled like a headmaster's study. The choirmaster, a talented musician with a self-effacing manner and boyish looks, had a flock of (white) adopted daughters and a wife we were afraid of because then no one really explained to children why people might be in a wheelchair, that they were just like everyone else inside. I think she was a nice, interesting woman, but I don't know, because I don't think my mother ever saw past the wheelchair, nor perhaps did many of the other women connected to the church. They all wore woollen coats, with gloves and hats; on rainy Sundays they smelled like a flock of sheep.

I liked singing among adults, serious stuff, no jingles, four parts. The men wore suits and ties. The choir filed into church through a secret door, and lined themselves up on a two-tiered, velvet-cushioned bench that arched round the proscenium of the church, looking down with tilted heads and, it seemed to me then, sad adult eyes, on the minister as he preached. Perhaps, like my own mother, who never joined the choir, they were actually thinking, Get a move on, I've a roast in the oven. The choirmaster sat in a sunken pit at the organ, a magnificent instrument whose pipes were up behind us. The pipes seemed to me, when I was a small child, like a giant box of jumbo pencils, some of which had been sharpened more often than others. The organist would conduct the choir with that wonderful ease and control of a competent keyboard player who keeps his voices or instruments with him – I remember seeing Daniel Barenboim doing it one evening in 1989, at a hastily organised concert to celebrate the fall of the Berlin Wall. With our downcast Modigliani gazes fixed on him we would sing, 'Draw nigh to God, and He will draw nigh to you.'

The organist played alone at the end, when the choir had gathered in their scores and were sitting chatting, leaning across each other, laughing now, forgetting the roast dinners, readjusting their hats. My parents used to make a respectful point of sitting listening, like people staying to watch the credits at the end of a film, even the one for the second props adviser. Usually it was either Bach's 'Toccata and Fugue' or Widor's toccata. My mother loved both, but I didn't feel up to playing either of them at her funeral, and they would have been too grand anyway. Instead I played 'To a Wild Rose' by Edward MacDowell on a sturdy upright piano with a few sticky notes – thorns, she would have said.

The church was not a beautiful building, but it was in the right place, at the heart of the village, on a central square. The total separation of Church and school in France, however, has led to several generations growing up thinking of it as a sinister and antiquated institution where only extremists, losers and people in distress hang out. Since the Second World War spirituality has moved house, resurfacing mostly in groups agitating for social and environmental change, alternative medicine and anti-racism. The Church has blotted its copybook too often: too many mistakes in transcription and interpretation have occurred; the original, simple message has been all but totally obscured.

For a long time I thought of the meeting of the vernacular Bible and the printing press as a great and liberating thing, and of course it was; but the spread of the Word Comprehensible in written form probably also led to some entrenchment and atrophy, blocking off the possibility of renewal and change. The artist and the sculptor are freer with their interpretations. Versions and variations abound. The printed word is a peculiarly patriarchal instrument. If the Church had never had a written liturgy, its books of stories, its letters and codified doctrines, would it have been less susceptible to corruption? At least in Chinese Whispers everyone knows and accepts that the message is evolving all the time. Where the message is written down, the ink dry on the page, immutable word of the Father, it quickly becomes a tool of oppression.

But prejudice of any kind is distressing, and the prejudice against the Church in France is so flagrant it makes you want to dust off your missal and go and support it, like some ailing football club. And ailing it is. Some writers have suggested that in France the all-but-disappearance of the Church as a serious adversary accounts for an increase in Islamophobia among modern rational secularists – *à la recherche de l'adversaire perdu.*

I was interested, too, in the Virgin Mary. I wanted to know what she had to say to a modern mother. Julia Kristeva says that today motherhood is imbued with what

remains of religious feeling, that the awe and piety sur-
rounding motherhood is religious sensibility's final refuge.
I saw Mary as a symbol of motherhood. I really felt for her,
the way Jesus was constantly batting her away: 'Did you not
know I would be in my Father's house?' I was aware that the
myth of her virginity rests on a mistranslation of the word
parthenos, more correctly meaning 'young maiden'. None of
that mattered too much to me, although as a translator of
literary fiction it encouraged me to double-check my proofs.
From such 'creative acts of infidelity' giant dogmas grow.

I had a sneaking sense of transgression when, at the end
of each service, the congregation sang, '*Sainte Marie, mère de
Dieu, priez pour nous, pauvres pécheurs.*' I had learned as a child
to address my thoughts directly to God, to go straight to the
headmaster. Occasionally you spoke to the deputy, with his
more human face, but there were no deputy headmistresses,
not even in the image of Miss Bowen, who was head of girls
at my grammar school, and the subject of whose virginity
was certainly never raised. I knew all this was ridiculous,
but I also knew that it was possible to short-circuit all the
personifications and go straight to the faintly beating heart
of the world, be reconnected in stillness with what it meant
to be human, through meditation, prayer and the candid
recognition of one's own failures, without harping on at it
and getting hung up about marks. And that through doing
so it was possible to be re-energised in one's belief that good
should and could be done, that the world might be trans-
formed for the better and that one might be a minuscule,
ant-like agent of it. That a life could be worse spent.

So after a while I went to church, approaching it sideways, through music, and the children occasionally came

with me. On her ninth birthday Clara was actually baptised a Catholic. I didn't want to have her baptised when she was a baby, even though some people suggested there was a particular urgency. But now she was older and was interested in religion – particularly in angels and the beautiful paintings in the art books in the attic. The Mayor's wife, an angelic atheist who cared devotedly for her own ailing mother, was restoring a small lady-chapel in the church and taught the children to draw and paint on Wednesday afternoons. They disappeared on their scooters to her studio and spent hours there with friends, experimenting with colours and creating circuses and theatres peopled with tiny humans, some with wings, with animals and talking teapots. Her triptych in the lady-chapel showed the Annunciation in one panel, Mary telling her news to her cousin Elizabeth in the middle panel, and the nativity in the third, all in bold vermillion, cerulean and gold. Each of the paintings explicitly set the scene in the village, with the characteristic features of the landscape and even the church itself in the background. The children made little distinction between fairies, angels, saints, animals round the crib, the Virgin Mary, the bishop, the priest. They were all characters, good subjects for a picture. They were less interested in Jesus: they couldn't quite get the sense of him. This was because most images of him showed him being crucified. The priest says that when he sees Christ on the cross he sees not a depiction of a man being tortured, but the triumph of love over suffering. I am not sure he should be the judge of that.

On the path that ran along beside the river was a small chapel, the size of a kitchen and the shape of a boat. When we asked if Clara could be baptised there, the priest said no, she had to do it like everyone else, in church, in front of the congregation she was to become part of. We were allowed a blessing in the chapel. Nico read from *Le Petit Prince*, some friends who were coming back from the gardens left their bicycles on the grass and came in, the Mayor's wife came in too because she loved the children and they her. Clara's friend Alice, the daughter of one of her godfathers, read a prayer that said, 'May the roof never fall in and may we never fall out,' a blessing on friendship. That morning Alice, Clara and her godparents jumped off the bridge to celebrate her birthday. The priest didn't come; I think he saw our wanting a private service in a place with a picturesque history by the river as a kind of religious tourism, and the service was led by a deacon. Even the new priest who arrived a year later refused to baptise Verity when we asked him, saying she had to have two years of catechism under her belt first. We were definitely not serious Christian parents.

On ordinary Sundays I played the harmonium at the front of the church, under the eye of the priest. As I pedalled away, playing jaunty 1960s settings of the Mass, I could feel the Blessed Agathe wincing at my shoulder – a young nun who had been born locally, refused to renounce her faith and been guillotined. She and her fellow nuns were transported to their deaths through the streets of Paris in a handcart, singing. She was beatified in the 1960s and is remembered reverently by the churchgoers in the village, most of whom are, as elsewhere, over seventy-five.

Agathe's story reminded me of a tale I loved as a child: a man fell asleep in a church service one very hot day. He dreamed that he was at the scaffold on the place de la Révolution, about to be guillotined. His wife, noticing he was asleep, tapped him on the back of the neck with her fan. He died on the spot. The point was, you had to identify the flaw in the story. In a novel I never finished I had a character put the riddle to her cousin on a harvest-festival Sunday morning.

'You're meant to say,' she explained, 'that it can't be true because you could never know what he had been dreaming.' It was an unsatisfying solution to a non-problem. It was all the wrong way round. The story should not have been told in the first place if you could not know what anyone was thinking. You had no business saying anything about anything. You could only say, 'A man was sitting in church with his wife and fell asleep.' You could never make anything up. It would be a very restricting way to live.

A very restricting way to write, too. I puzzled over it during prayers. My words flew up, my thoughts remained below.

For weddings and funerals and special days in the Church calendar I went up the back stairs into the organ loft. It was a discreet place from which to watch the goings-on during the Mass. It is difficult to stand and say the Creed when you are perched on a tiny organ bench up in a kind of crow's nest at the west end of the church. I liked to pretend I was walking in the steps of Albert Schweitzer – he played the organ at Saint-Sulpice when he was a student in Paris, and in the jungle in Gabon he had a three-pedalled piano specially made so he could play his Bach in the early hours of the morning. The extra pedal made it possible for him to sustain notes indefinitely, as on the organ. It was this particular feature of the instrument that led Charles-Marie Widor, Schweitzer's teacher, to say that the organ playing was 'the manifestation of a will filled with the vision of eternity'. I have a *faiblesse* for Schweitzer that goes back to my childhood. Take away the proselytisers' wilful distortions and the natural evolution of the various species of truth that religion has put forward over the millennia, and Schweitzer's ethic of reverence for life, the belief that 'good consists in maintaining, assisting and enhancing life, and to destroy, to harm or to hinder life is evil', seems like a good place to start over. Except, of course, if you include bacteria. (I interpreted Schweitzer's ethic to mean life-with-consciousness.)

The staircase up to the organ loft was deep in bat droppings, and I always wore old clothes, even for weddings, because whatever I wore had to go straight in the washing machine afterwards. Bat droppings are rich in the microbe *Pseudomonas aeruginosa*, which is particularly dangerous for the lungs of someone with CF. Everywhere I was on the lookout for pseudomonas. Sometimes I thought that if had been religious I might have suspected God of testing me, or sending me messages. Even without being religious I was always receiving them: *Go and play the organ in the house of the God you no longer believe in, but beware of the bat droppings!* It was as though what I might be punished for was not lack of belief but an inability to shed it, as though God was tired of being believed in and would prefer no longer to be loved. After all, parents are supposed to want their children to leave home. Clara only once came up to the organ loft, to sing for a wedding. She sang Howard Goodall's setting of 'The Lord Is My Shepherd' for a French couple who worked

in Tower Bridge and wanted something English, and I realised halfway through, at 'Yea, though I walk in death's dark
vale', that I had forgotten about the bat droppings. Oh well,
fear no evil, I thought, and ploughed on. But at the next
examination, two weeks later, pseudomonas showed up in
her lungs. That taught me.

Ellie says to me, 'Grandma, I'll help you remember. I'll help you find your keys and your handbag. Then we can go out to the park and the shops. We can catch a bus and go and watch the ships come in.'

But where are my keys and my handbag? And where is the bus stop? I forget. I think I'm beginning to forget everything.

I stare at Ellie as if I'm not quite sure who she is, and she throws her arms around me and says, 'Oh Grandma, please remember. Please, please remember me.'

Margaret Wild, *Remember Me*

My mother's attitude to illness was thought by my father to have been passed down through her family. They were always, he said, 'taking to their beds'. Staying in bed was considered rather continental and louche. My grandmother, and occasionally my mother, given half a chance, napped after lunch, and he was bothered by this willing, even gleeful withdrawal, however brief, from the concerns of the world. After her marriage my mother began to hide any illness, to deny it wherever possible. Many a time she got up and cooked breakfast, fully dressed, pretending all was well, then went back to bed when we left for school and work.

For several months after Clara was diagnosed with cystic fibrosis I was told not to mention it to my father's sister, although she had a severe lung disease herself and knew all about CF from her monthly check-ups in the respiratory wing of the Sheffield Infirmary. She had been tested for it and the test had shown up negative. But it now seems quite likely that people who showed up on tests as having only one copy of a defective gene often did have two, one from each parent, but one of the pair was of such a rare type that it wasn't tested for. It might give you some symptoms, but in genetic testing it wouldn't show up.

I think possibly that Auntie Dorothy had cystic fibrosis, with one Delta F508 gene (Clara had two) and another, rarer modifying one. I have learned a lot since the days when, in Mr Tranter's biology class, we copied down notes off the blackboard about Mendel's peas. I am still surprised that in the years since Clara was diagnosed, none of my family – brother, parents, cousins, second cousins, aunts, uncles – has chosen to be tested for CF. I have no idea to this day which side of my family it comes from.

In the early days of my mother's illness, before we really understood what it would mean, we were driving home from a visit to Auntie Dorothy, with Clara sleeping in the baby seat beside my mother in the back. I said, 'I don't understand why you don't want me to tell her.'

My mother looked fixedly out of the window, as though the passing cooling towers had a greater claim on her interest. When I looked back at the road she said in a pious little voice I didn't recognise, 'Some things are just best kept to ourselves.'

'You mean we're supposed to pretend?' I think at the time I wanted the world to know. I couldn't help myself telling people. Perhaps I hoped that one day someone unexpected would say, 'You know they can cure that, haven't you heard?' Or else I never wanted to be in the situation of being told about it again, of having it sprung on me. So I would pre-empt, by doing the telling myself. It was an expression my grandmother used a lot: 'She won't be told!'

My mother went on in the same strange, high, teacherly, preacherly voice, 'I do not consider it appropriate that we tell her at this time.'

'What?'

She settled her hands, almost as though in prayer, primly on her lap. 'I just wouldn't wish . . . to up*set* her.'

She began to hum, and if I say it was a hymn people will think it's just a cheap jibe, but she actually did. She who had often gone to church reluctantly, and baulked at all the silly pettiness and wished she could just go for a walk up a mountain and maybe meet God somewhere up there, forgot everything about religion as she slid into dementia, everything but the pieties that had most irritated her.

'You're saying she has an illness that's unspeakable, that people shouldn't have to know about. In case it's too painful for them. For *them*!'

'Don't shout, dear, you'll wake the baby.'

'Clara, her name's Clara!'

'That's as may be, but she's only a baby.'

'What do you mean, "That's as may be"? What kind of an expression is that? *It's her name*!'

'That's enough!' she barked, as though on a parade ground, which I think she had been once or twice, when she spent a brief spell in the air force. It made a huge impression on her speech habits. 'You're getting hysterical. Look, you've gone and woken her now.' She looked sideways at the baby. It was a mean, knowing look, which seemed to say, 'I always suspected, but now I know, your mother's a right bitch.' Except that wasn't at all the kind of relationship we'd had, or the kind of thing she would ever have thought. I didn't understand about Alzheimer's. I thought she didn't want to tell the 'Sheffield relatives' because she was afraid they'd turn Clara's illness into a hospital drama, an episode of *Casualty*. There was some sense in that. Clara started crying. I pulled over on to the hard shoulder. 'For goodness' sake! You're overreacting,' my mother shouted, then slumped back in her seat. Clara yelled louder. I got out and opened the back door, undid Clara's straps and plucked her out, got back into the driver's seat and put her on my breast. 'I never did that with you,' my mother said mildly. She seemed to have forgotten that we had

59

just been shouting at each other. 'You didn't care for it. I tried, but you wouldn't. Oh-ho-no! You liked your bottle.'

I said again, 'I would just like not to be secretive. About her illness.'

'Don't fuss, dear. They all have these little ailments. With your first you always panic. Think they're going to die when it's just a little wind! Ridiculous really!' She put her head between the front seats, the way we used to on long car journeys when we were children, hoping for toffees or mints, and looked down at Clara. 'Is that it, darling? Just a little bit of wind in your little tummy?'

My tears fell down on to Clara's cheek. 'She can die. Children do die of it.'

'Nonsense,' she said, 'not from a bit of trapped wind. She's a strong healthy girl!'

'But she's not,' I said. 'She weighs four kilos and she's eight months old.'

'Well if you will go talking in *kilos*!'

I was so tired, so unbelievably tired with it all. 'We cannot expect her to live beyond thirty. Unless they find a cure.'

'Oh, hush,' she said, 'you'll go frightening her.'

'No I won't,' I said. 'She doesn't understand yet.' Though I had imagined the day when she would, when I would have to explain. They said in the hospital that by the time I came round to explaining I would discover she already knew, like puberty.

Clara had fallen asleep. I brought her back and strapped her in again. Now I saw my mother was crying, her lips all shaky, as though there was no muscle in them. She was wiping her nose on her sleeve. She told me once that at school, in Liverpool during the war, if you cried they called you a

'silversleeves'. She looked at me piteously. The car kept rocking as lorries floundered by. She gripped her seat, the way she
had when I was first learning to drive. Where was my mother,
I thought. I need my mother! Not you. You're no use to me.
No use to anyone.

'I'm just a poor, weak old lady,' she said in a teeny-tiny
voice. 'Take me home now. I don't understand anything.
Daddy will be cross!

'Cwoss!' she repeated in a baby voice. 'Daddy will be so
cwoss!' But she said it very quietly, aware that it would actually
be Daughter who'd be *cwoss*.

When we got off the motorway and stopped at the traffic
lights, I turned round and looked down at Clara. She was sitting in her little seat, looking at my mother cannily, as though
assessing a suspicious stranger in the cinema. Her eyes took up
most of her face. 'Sharp as a tack, that one,' a man had said to
me in a café. My mother turned to her and winked and said,
in a grown-up voice this time, 'Wide awake now, are we?'
She looked back out of the window at the artificial lake with
giant hoardings inviting people to take a leap and relocate to
rural Doncaster. 'I do that sometimes. I knew you were just
pretending. Got you taped.' After we'd gone round several
roundabouts, past Asda and the Outlet and the bowling and
ice rinks, I said, 'I'm sorry you're upset. It doesn't matter
now.'

She exhaled slowly, smoothed her skirt. Then she shook
herself out of character, looked up at me and said briskly, in
her normal voice, the voice that was her: 'That's OK, darling, I know I can be maddening. Let's forgive and forget,
shall we?'

I nodded, and moved back into the outer lane.

'I'll tell you what, though,' she said. 'You've forgotten to stop at Asda for the bread.'

I smiled weakly. I'd always been the forgetful one in the family. I'd lost more credit cards and sets of house keys than anyone I knew, or than anyone known to anyone I knew. Our eyes met in the mirror, and she looked away first. 'You'll be forgetting your own name next,' she prophesied.

Between the boards a strip of fresh deep blue was showing, against which the little lamp seemed to make a red stain. The dawn was breaking.

The old woman slowly drew her fingers out of the man's hand, and placed one upon her lips.

'*À ce moment de sa narration*,' she said, '*Scheherazade vit paraître le matin, et, discrète, se tut.*'

Isak Dinesen, *Seven Gothic Tales*

My mother was inordinately fond of a film she'd seen once in Wigan, at the Ritzy or the Roxy, called *Le Ballon Rouge*. She worked as a newly qualified history mistress in a girls' school there in the 1950s, lodging with three old ladies who, she said, were straight out of *Arsenic and Old Lace*. I accepted these cinematic references without any sense that these were films one might ever see. They were evanescent, one-off events in my mother's life, part of no other canon but hers. I first saw *The Red Balloon* on video, ordered from Amazon, when my children were very small and my mother had dementia and sat unblinking, unrecognising as the cherished images flicked by. It has almost no dialogue, but a delightful score, strings and accordion immediately evoking the smell of scorching rubber, roast chicken, bread, whatever Paris smells like to you. A small boy meets a red balloon, which follows him wherever he goes, on the tram to school, into the *boulangerie*. When necessary it waits outside, hovering nonchalantly in the air. Sometimes the boy takes it by the string, where its hand would be if it was a person, sometimes the balloon just follows after. In the final part of the film the boy is taken to Mass at Sacré-Coeur by his grandmother. He takes the balloon along with him, but the balloon is told to wait outside by a sidesman or church steward. Bad idea. The balloon gets frisky, waiting. The little boy skips Mass and comes back out into the street. Soon he is seen fleeing a gang of boys, who chase him through the city to a place of high ground, where they attack him and puncture the balloon. At the moment when the balloon succumbs to the bullies' stabbing, all the balloons in Paris, red, green, blue, yellow, orange, slip from their tethers and whizz through the air, joining in the end to form a glorious cluster of colour. The boy is lifted up into the skies by the balloons. There are Christian echoes in this persecution and elevation, but I think they are no more than echoes and that the filmmaker is tapping a powerful associative stream in our brains. He is not actually saying anything about Christianity, just using its clothing to move us where we can effectively be moved.

On the first day of our family trip to Paris, when I was nine, we climbed the steps to Sacré-Coeur, which I knew wasn't made of icing, but which appealed to me more than Notre-Dame because it looked as though it might be. It was Friday afternoon. We had woken up in Doncaster and flown in a draughty charter plane. But here in this country it was Paris, as though Paris was just a time of day, or a day of the week. We entered the cathedral, which inside was dark and full of chambers, niches, not at all like the bleached schoolrooms of Methodism. We re-emerged and against an azure sky a great bubble of coloured balloons flew. Ah, my mother said, 'Ah, le ballon rouge,' and her voice lifted as she told us the story.

My mother was not a natural inventor of stories, more of a fabricator, a spinner. Often her stories became stories about telling stories. We'd be waiting in the car for my father to emerge from a meeting, with his Bible under his arm, and one of us would ask for a story. She'd sigh and say, at first, with little interest and almost by way of refusal: 'It was a dark and stormy night, and the captain said to Antonio, "Antonio, tell us a story." And Antonio began: "It was a dark and stormy night . . . "'

But, as this was not much of a story to keep children entertained, slowly, brightening at the idea of deviation, she would embroider once the first telling was done and she had limbered up, saying: 'It was a dark and stormy night, and the pirate ship rocked on the waters of a southern ocean. Their voyage home, after looting the furthermost island of the archipelago Forlorna, where for decades the native people had hoarded the lost treasure of *Sally Green*, a Bristol-built schooner lost in the reign of William and Mary, drew from the weary crew every last ounce of stamina and endurance. On that night, half the crew were sick with food poisoning – the ship's cook's cat had infected flea bites, and the malady was spreading from the galleys upwards – and the captain was concerned for his motley gang, who, had history been different, might have grown to the respectable estate of doctors, lawyers, politicians or country curates with pretty wives. And so, seeking to distract them from their sorry state, he turned to Antonio, a young man discovered in a basket among bulrushes on the island and raised by a missionary's unmarried daughter, and said: "Antonio, Antonio, tell us a story." And Antonio began: "It was a dark and stormy night, and the pirate ship rocked on the waters of a southern ocean . . ."' But already at the second telling it was a perilous narrative undertaking. The story, elaborate as it had now become, was impossible to remember. There were multiple errors and omissions along the way. And each time she would include still more material, inserting new adjectives as her story ripened, new descriptive sub-clauses, new considerations of the socio-political misfortunes of minor characters. So each nested version of the story was different, as probably oral stories were before it became common to record them as text. It was an important moment in the history of humanity, when the first scribe served the first oral poet. Early medieval texts recording popular love stories or tales of chivalry in war contain many repetitions and refrains, and follow strict metric patterns, reflecting the heavy use of mnemonics by the oral poets. But my mother's tales were the oral tales of someone who had always read books. You need to write such stories down, or be prepared to lose them on the high seas of what literary theorists call 'reception'. My mother's tale soon faltered, and the story would head off around the world, which was after all round, returning no doubt in the end to Bristol Docks, point of repair and restructure, and new departures. She was able to embroider because her brain was a storehouse of memories – of episodes, places, moods, incidents, characters, concepts, colours – to which, back then, she still had open access.

Over the last ten years I have translated from French into English the works of Congolese novelist Alain Mabanckou, all of them first-person narratives in the '*je*' voice of either the author/narrator or of other characters into whose skin Mabanckou is adept at stepping (even, in one case, in the voice of an animal double, a wily porcupine). But no text can ever, or should, be a completely faithful transcription of an oral telling. What you try to render, as author and as translator, is the tipping moment, just as the spoken word dries on the page. This, the outer message, is vulnerable to 'damage' by the typographer and printer, editor and translator – whose concentration may occasionally waver, though rarely to the point of introducing changes of meaning. Sometimes these lapses might be Freudian, or raise a wry smile, but mostly they belong to the category of minor joke. Can the inclusion in the so-called 'Wicked Bible' of 'Thou shalt commit adultery' really have led generations of the faithful astray?

Once the story enters the reader's consciousness, though, the cage door is wide open again, and there is no controlling the tale that has been set free of the printed page. Just as the teller is able to draw on her brain store to embroider and elaborate, select and dramatise, so, once the tale is told and the outer message has delivered its inner message, the listener or reader gets to work on it, and the meaning is scrambled, mirrored, contorted, deepened by the refracting process that takes place in the brain.

Similarly with music. Musicians working from a score are translators. They translate the signs into sound; and I use the word 'translate' not in the Google Translate sense, but to mean that series of infinitely careful, occasionally inspired judgements that allows the writer's original choice of words to dance as unfettered as it did that first time on the page, so that the language of the translation is almost transparent. But musicians do more than translate. They interpret the signs, and beyond them the intentions of the composer – trying, indeed, to get past the signs, the aide-memoire, to the sound in the composer's head, to render it anew. No one performer or translator ever makes quite the same choices. The discrepancies between the interpretations of individual musicians/translators attest not only to their level of skill but also to the climatic and historic conditions in their brains that have led them to make their choices.

And the reader, too, is an *interprète*. Unconsciously, as she reads, her vast and highly personal memory store illuminates what is before her, and often projects on to it incidents in her own life, or in other books she has read, prejudices, convictions, fears and yearnings. The fertile and active process of mixing, matching and making fruitful with our perception of the outside world and our inner storehouse of memories and concepts – that is what scientists call 'consciousness'. It is a process that becomes increasingly restricted as access to the memory store declines with old age, particularly with dementia. Long after the names of everyday objects had gone, and notions like Christmas and Beethoven – 'Switch that off!' – my mother continued to tell the children the story of Mickey the chimp, which she'd been telling, Ancient Mariner-like, all my life.

She and her brother had grown up in Liverpool in the 1930s. My grandfather never had a very stable job. When he worked on the mail ships that sailed between Liverpool and New York, the Elder Dempster Lines, he would bring home fruit – green bananas, which my grandmother hung from the pulley above the range in the kitchen to ripen, and avocado pears. Once when the boat docked, a chimp disembarked. The mother chimp had been shot by white men, and this was one of her surviving babies. Mickey, as he became known, was kept in Liverpool Zoo, and my mother and her brother used to go and visit it after school. They built up a special relationship with the chimp. At the start of the war the children were sent away to north Wales, where my mother was put with one family and my uncle another. My mother did not thrive.

One day she was summoned to the headmistress's study. Along the corridor she went, rehearsing her excuses before she even knew what the charges might be. To her surprise my grandmother, big-boned, fair-haired, in an unprepossessing hat and coat and clutching an umbrella, was in the headmistress's study, as though this was a dream and the wrong people were in the wrong places. Grandma didn't like the tone of my mother's letters, particularly not the talk of bedbugs. No bombs had fallen, so she'd come to take the children home. After they returned to Liverpool, the bombs began to fall. Shortly before the primary school they attended was replaced by a hole in the ground, Mickey escaped from his cage and from the zoo, pushing his keeper out of the way, ripping the flesh on his shoulder. He lolloped down the streets and made his way to the school. He climbed up on to the roof. The children were marshalled into lines and marched back into the classroom. A sniper was sent for. But one boy's cap fell off and he dashed back into the middle of the yard to retrieve it. The chimp bounded down from the roof, swinging down the drainpipe, lunging for the cap. He snatched it up and was about to put it back on the boy's head in a gesture that would for ever be open to interpretation, having never been performed, when the sniper's bullet hit Mickey and he fell.

My mother told this story so many times, it became a habitual action, like making a cup of tea or folding laundry. It turned out slightly different every time, not so as you'd notice, just with a slight change of emphasis or twist. But as her mind declined she began to tell the story more and more fiercely, with odd interpolations which she insisted were true. It had happened to her. It had happened to her brother Ben. My grandfather had brought the chimp home. He'd slept in the children's bed. He'd slept in the kitchen. He wore little red shorts that my uncle had grown out of. He played the piano, 'Für Elise'. It was torment to my father, for whom fiction itself was problematic, because its propositions were untrue. My mother rattled on, repeating and repeating, coiling back on herself, unravelling, till the story acquired a kind of shrill and ragged brilliance. Usually he would leave the room or read the newspaper till his eyes burned the page. On the last occasion I ever heard her tell it, though, unable to bear the ending for the children, and the grim, heedless words that had only come in the most recent tellings, he swooped in at the close, just as she was about to assert that the carcass of the animal had been dragged across the playground, leaving a trail of blood as red as the dirt in Africa. 'But the sniper never came,' he told the children in a gentle voice. They looked at him as though he'd shone a light on them in the dark, their faces swivelling towards him in the sure and certain hope of deliverance. He shook his head slowly. 'No, he never came. So Mickey rounded up the children. To one he gave a trumpet, another a drum and two wooden sticks, another a triangle and another a little flag. And he marched them all out of the schoolyard and down Lime Street and to the docks, to catch a boat for Europe, to win the war against the enemy, and carry us all to glory, in a land of hope, without cruelty or pain.'

She is like a horse grazing
a hill pasture that someone makes
smaller by coming every night
to pull the fences in and in.

She has stopped running wide loops,
stopped even the tight circles.
She drops her head to feed; grass
is dust, and the creekbed's dry.

Master, come with your light
halter. Come and bring her in.

Jane Kenyon, 'In the Nursing Home'

When we moved to France I knew I would have to face my fear of air travel and go back to England to visit my parents every month, or at most every six weeks. I would drive to the airport, an hour from the village exactly, along country roads, through a landscape that did not cease to be my own until just a few miles short of the airport, so that it always came as a surprise to turn the corner and find the terminal, which seemed to have been towed out from the city, a temporary structure, like the hypermarkets and roundabouts on the edge of all French towns. It is only natural that houses built of local stone, stone by stone, should seem to have emerged from the earth like plants, and that structures made of brick, and subsequently other more complex materials, to have been flown in or towed out from some industrial site. One of the most striking things about the opening ceremony to the 2012 Olympics was this reminder that the industrial age was the age of the processing of raw materials in factories into high volumes of identical goods; the age of transformation, usually by means of the conversion of heat energy into brute force. The fruits of the Industrial Revolution I would find hardest to live without would be recorded music and medical care. But it's true that without a plane I could not have got back to see my mother every six weeks. I suppose I would not have left her in the first place. Maybe, without any of that, the area around Doncaster would have remained as it was in the time of the Pilgrim Fathers.

The little villages around where I grew up produced many dissenters. I began to write a novel set in the early seventeenth century, a squire and a clerk, perhaps, in a comfortable drawing room, with horses tethered at the gate, discussing matters of religion. A woman who does not want to leave her elderly parents. If she goes to the New World she will never see them again. And her children may get scurvy on the crossing, and die. They will go first to Leiden, after a midnight flit down the River Idle to the coast. In Leiden they will hear the music of Bach, and one of them, who can carry a tune, will take a version of a cantata in his head to the New World, to which they will sing grace before meals. It will not quite be Bach's version, but related to it.

Whenever I got to the airport and parked my car, I found myself disorientated and confused as I crossed over to the terminal building, wondering whether I too might be in the early stages of Alzheimer's. I found it difficult to observe the formalities of departure. *Enregistrement, embarquement.* Security. No matter how hard I tried, I was always carrying something forbidden; I just couldn't get my head round the restrictions. Could there be a category of people who find instructions and procedures difficult and who don't suffer from any known mental illness, who are just not good at processing that kind of information? If I had illicit tastes I'd be in prison the whole time.

At the other end, it was easier. I rarely had more than hand luggage anyway. This was that particular kind of travel, the kind undertaken by grown-up children to visit their parents, with a small bag and no special clothes. An ex-boyfriend once commented on my name: 'Helen: two parts heaven, one part hell.' He was a good writer, but tended to err, I felt, on the side of rancour. It would have been a good phrase to describe how I felt about those trips back to Yorkshire, though. Always that lift of happiness as I drove up the A1 in the evening, often with fields either side bathed in mellow light, and the soft babble of the radio I thought I had missed but, by the time I got to Stamford, or at most Grantham, tired of and switched off.

I love to drive north. Home is at the other end. Not in the sense of my home, but that sense Robert Frost pinpointed when he said, 'Home is the place where, when you have to go there,/They have to take you in.' Even later, when I knew I would find my mother sitting in a sodden armchair, masticating toothlessly, with her once-pretty fine brown hair standing in a startled grey thatch about her head, revealing her ears, which she always liked to cover save for just the lobes and the pretty clip-on earrings my father bought her on wedding anniversaries. And my father, almost helpless in the face of this thing he could not change, or control, or shape, or arrest, his wife's descent into madness. For a man who had ticked her off, the first time he and she went to stay with his parents in their council house on the edge of Sheffield, for not wearing gloves to church, to find her fifty years on in wet pants and with egg all down her shirt five minutes after he had changed and washed her was a version of the myth of Sisyphus that seemed specifically designed as a torture for him.

For a long time my mother lived at home and my father cared for her with the help of the social services and nursing agencies. Then she was admitted to hospital, and suddenly everything was out of our hands. She'd been admitted because a woman from the care agency we employed had insisted on her having a bath, and she'd fainted when the room became too hot. The woman from the care agency then insisted on the doctor being called, because she couldn't not report it, or she'd have been 'liable'. And then the doctor had insisted on her being hospitalised, even though he maybe should have used his common sense and seen that she needed to be left at home in a bed in a room she might just recognise, some of the time. I hated going to see her in the hospital. I asked Clara's consultant the other day if he didn't mind working in a hospital. 'No,' he said, 'but if my child was sick, or I was, I would feel just like you.' Everyone on my mother's side of the family had always hated hospitals. But everyone on my father's side, except my father himself – who considered even his own hypochondria an affliction serious enough to kill him – seemed to love the world of the ward and the nurses and the cosiness, and the remedies for ills that came in the form of little white tablets in brown, semi-transparent bottles. As a child I always associated hospitals with dying, largely perhaps because my other, Scottish, grandmother was in hospital in Blackpool in the 1970s when the son of the Grand Mufti of Jerusalem entered the ward and stabbed five children and two nurses. For the first few years of Clara's life I associated them with alienation, and the loss of yourself, and potentially lethal germs and people telling my daughter, 'This won't hurt,' meaning 'It will hurt, but you've been warned.'

Visiting my mother one evening, I tried parking my father's car in one of the side streets near the hospital, because unless you arrived before opening hours, you couldn't get a parking space. I had done my driving lessons round the infirmary, and gone to sleazy parties in the converted front rooms of absent parents when I was in the sixth form. It is amazing what you can do with a few joss sticks, candles, 'Stairway to Heaven' and boys and girls scattered over the floor like animal rugs.

The parking space was barely longer than the car, but by reversing and advancing and reversing and advancing I managed to squeeze into it. I walked unsteadily down the street, crossed the main road and entered the hospital.

She's on the thirteenth floor, on a ward with other old people, in bed by the window. She clutches at my hand. I squeeze her hand so hard she yelps, then strokes my hand better. 'So sorry, darling. Where am I? Can I go home?' There is real terror in her face. 'Can I go home soon? Can I go home soon? Can I go home?'

I look out on the Middle England spread of streets, the parish church and the cooling towers, the head of the mine-shaft and pit wheel, the race-course pavilion where we went (no betting that day, so OK) to play in the wind band for when the Queen came, and where we once attended an Ideal Homes exhibition and a 'dodgy character with the gift of the gab' sold my mother an 'autocutter' for chopping vegetables. And the town playing fields with the grammar school on the north side, where my mother came to watch me play hockey, and on one occasion picked me and my friend up on a long-distance run and deposited us in record-breaking time back at school, where the games mistress was found drinking coffee in the staffroom with her legs up on a table. On occasions Arthur Scargill and Joe Gormley would come and watch us too. I think they met on the touchline of the hockey pitch because they thought MI6 were bugging them. Happy days. Well, not very happy, actually. (My mother wrote in her diary for 16 September 1989, when I got married, not for long: *Happy day.* Then added, years later, when she could barely write but had attained a greater sense of realism, *Not really.*) I hated being made to act the part of the games mistress in *The Happiest Days of Your Life* in the second year at secondary school. It was like having my grandmother hovering over us at teatime in winter, with the smell of the gas fire making us sick and dull-witted, saying in a voice as sweet as her scented hand cream, 'You *love* your Spam, don't you?'

I reminded my mother of things like this. She patted my hand, as though it was me that was raving. 'Can I go home now?'

I asked the nurses. 'Can she come home?' They were doing nothing here, except increasing her sense of alienation and hastening her dive into full-scale dementia. I could see her about to flop, belly-first like a great walrus, into a warm sea from which there was no return. 'You'll have to stop in while Monday. When the doctor comes!' they shouted at her. She opened her eyes very wide, and shrank back slightly against the pillow on the stalk of her neck. 'Stay in,' she said, stiffly. '*Till* Monday.' Then, to me: 'Can I go home now? Can I go home?'

Eventually I said I had to go. She waved me away. '"Stand not upon the order of your going,"' she said, '"But go at once."' When the Methodist minister came to visit her and prayed with her, she looked squarely at him after his 'Amen' and said, '"My words fly up, my thoughts remain below./ Words without thoughts never to heaven go."'

I came out, like so many, in tears, crossing the car park with an empty feeling in my chest, which, metaphor would have it, was because I had left my heart inside with her. But it wasn't really a metaphor, or at least only the bit equating the heart with the fullness and centre of the emotions. And yet I had my family to get back to, my father to clean and cook and shop for, though he was getting increasingly adept

78

at that; my husband and daughters in France: my daughter to care for and hydrate and feed with high-fat food and get to the physio and fill with medicines, and the little one, Verity, to produce some semblance of a normal childhood for. Like so many people – the majority, probably – I felt the circumstances of my life were quite extreme. I got back to the car, and climbed inside. A man came dashing out from a house and banged on the window. When I opened it, he shouted at me for parking so tight he couldn't move his own car. 'Are you mad?' he yelled. I had manoeuvred myself skilfully into a position from which I couldn't exit without causing and sustaining damage.

Shortly after that she went into the home and my father visited her every single day for several hours, except for the occasions when he flew to France to spend a few days with us. When we all come over to visit her, Clara goes straight up and embraces her, wrapping her arms around her, rubbing her nose up and down my mother's dried-petal cheek. Verity, who never overstates or understates, whose name could not be more her own, leans her back against the wall and slides down, slowly, unobtrusively to the carpet, watching silently over the top of her folded arms, which slightly shield her face. My mother says things like 'I'm going to die soon. The thought gives me no pleasure, but I've had a lovely time.'

She also says, one afternoon:

'I know we all die
But we will come to life again
And we will love each other
As much as we do now.

'We both lived here
Between 3 and 4
But we'll come back to life again.
I'll see you tomorrow.
Goodnight.

'Oh, we'll last for a long time.
We're both alive.
There's today in life
And there's the life after.
Both are equally important.
Goodnight.

'Theoretically I'm dead and buried.
But not really, dear.
We've got our whole life to come.
Goodnight.'

All her life she had wanted to write, but all her starts were false, or they were true to start with but then she had to go back again, letting her ink dry, always fearful of the eye over her shoulder. Released from the straitjacket of the need to '*bien écrire*', she seemed to lapse into profundity.

I tend to agree with the theory that if you want to keep a memory pristine, you must not call upon it too often, for each time it is revisited, you alter it irrevocably, remembering not the original impression left by experience but the last time you recalled it. With tiny differences creeping in at each cycle, the exercise of our memory does not bring us closer to the past but draws us further away.

Sally Mann, *Hold Still: A Memoir with Photographs*

Trees in full leaf line the route of the river, which rushes busily beneath an iron bridge. Not the prettiest bridge. Somewhere below, the stumps of the medieval bridge squat, and the slurry water close to the river bed swells round them. In summer the children, young and old, take leaps from the bridge into the water. They are not leaping into the water, they are leaping into space, knowing the water will catch them. They know where the old bridge stumps sit on the riverbed, and jump between them. For fish it must be like swimming through an ancient marketplace, with colonnades. Water-skiers skim up and down the river in August, when the promenade turns Parisian and boats are moored all the length of it. Young men with lean torsos grapple with engines, and the children dance around on the quay in their blue, green, red and orange swimsuits, legs brown and feet bare, like little ice-cream cornets. The pizza café is open on the quay two months of the year. Late in the evening I walk out with the dog and stop and talk to people I know. These are days of rest. Often the children – not ours – are staying with grandparents, and the parents linger in the cafés, and walk, and take the time to argue and make up while the children are gone. The clink of cutlery and glasses and the almost insolent sound of laughter dies down around midnight. People trail home slowly, checking the moon for signs of a change in the weather. A Dutchman swipes the sky with his phone and tries to attract a woman's attention with his constellation app, but she laughs and waves him away.

The swimming instructor, Jérôme, is out late, and will be up again early in the morning. He calls to us as we walk by the café tables. The children are ahead with the dog. There is no time like the present, like now, I think; there is no time *but* the present, but now. In the dark like this, the half-lit, friendly dark that does not hide the world, only softens it, I lose my fears. Clara seems so light and quick. She loves to stay up late. Her sister is tired from swimming and cycling and late-night eating. Clara lifts her arms and swirls in a pool of light from a lamp on a neighbour's wall. Jérôme points over to a couple sitting finishing their meal. These are his friends from Lyon, with their child, a four-year-old girl. She has the same condition as Clara. They will not allow her to swim. The father will not speak about the illness. The mother does all the hospital visits, gives her all her medicines, does the physiotherapy. The father is still stunned, two years after the diagnosis. He is already mourning her, anticipating her absence, when she is taken from him before he is ready. 'Speak to them,' Jérôme urges.

So we go over and speak to them, reassure them. I try to pass on the word of faith that was given to me: 'She will be OK.' I am not given to glib reassurances; I say this believing it to be true. We describe how we travel with Clara, how she swims and water-skis, runs cross-country, sings, camps. We live a normal life, we say, then we both frown, because of course we don't, but we lead our life *plus* the normal one, with things taken out that we aren't allowed to do, and many things added to keep her safe. No wonder we are often tired. Clara asked me, when she was three, 'Do we all die?' and I said, 'Yes, but usually, if we are lucky, only when we are very tired and ready to go.' I believed this, too, because it was what my grandmother had told me. My cousin said, 'Don't say that: you're *always* tired!'

We don't really live a normal life, it is less spontaneous than other people's. We have to plan everything round Clara's treatments and state of health, which often, in the summer, is not so good. I feel like a seamstress who pins and tacks every seam, every hemline, and leaves the tacking in in case she has to unpick it and do it again, over and over. The children come up. The woman scrutinises Clara, who looks fine, if a little exotic in her different-coloured silk scarves and at least two dresses, worn one over the other. They like to dress up in the evening, like southern women: they have an inborn sense of the *passeggiata*, and their room, when they finally go to bed, looks as though some potentate's wife or diva has ripped through Liberty with her personal shopper and only half an hour to shop in. I kiss them below their eyes. It is a habit that comes from never wanting to kiss Clara on the lips, for fear of transmitting something to her. So I kiss them below the eyes, just underneath their cheekbones, and it feels more intimate even than a kiss pressed on to their lips. I close their shutters against the moon, but they don't close properly because they are warped and buckled and the iron pegs have rusted, and the moon slides in between them and places a silver sword on the crumpled pile of silks and discarded dresses between their beds.

That night the two waitresses from the pizza restaurant go out in a boat, after service is over and the kitchen cleared, with the pizza maker and the Spanish teacher from the primary school. Lying in bed I hear shouts, perhaps around two in the morning, cries like an animal's or a bird's, and I think perhaps I have misheard, that that is what it was. Very soon a silence falls. Most of us sleep. In the morning the quay is busy with men in dark blue and red preparing to dive for a body. The pizza maker fell off the back of the boat when it accelerated. The girls were at the front, the teacher at the back with the engine. How could no one have noticed when he fell? He was wearing a leather jacket; he couldn't swim. There is a post-mortem once the body is found, which delays the funeral and reveals nothing. There is no investigation, no one is accused of anything. The café closes for two days.

The day before the funeral, Laure, a singer who knows the family, calls me and asks me to play for the service. The family are not religious but she has suggested to the mother that they have a funeral in the church in their hamlet, a tiny stone building in a nest of streets on the top of a hill. Laure says, 'Right now she doesn't want to bury him, and certainly not with prayers, but later it will help her if she does.'

On the morning of the funeral Laure and I drive to the church and rehearse. It is difficult to play on the harmonium in a manner that isn't comic, but I have more or less got the hang of it now, and can produce a reedy noise which is plangent and not too like a hurdy-gurdy. I play very simple two-note chords for her while she sings 'Oh, Freedom'.

'And before I'll be a slave I'll be buried in my grave
And go home to my lord and be free.'

It is so beautiful, I say she should just sing it unaccompanied, and in the event she does, as the men come in with the coffin, out of the blazing sun on the white stone into the darkness of the chapel, itself cut into rock, but cool and feeling like a haven.

She does it so well, so simply, I can feel the strength of the music, and the ancient, many-times-repeated lyrics flow into the bereaved family. The mother looks like a Brechtian figure, haggard, not so very old; this is the second son she has lost, the previous one to an overdose. At the sound of Laure's voice she lifts her head and holds it high, as though displaying it to the watching mourners, as though it bears a disfigurement of which she has finally decided not to be ashamed. The preacher says, 'It seems to you that he has left you too early; but time is not the same for God. Perhaps God felt he had done what he had to do in this life.' It seems quite an unusual sentiment from a priest.

After the service people follow the coffin through the narrow streets down to the churchyard, a good twenty minutes' walk in the sun, but almost everyone goes, hundreds of them, most of whom weren't able to fit in the church. I don't go, because I didn't know the man, but later, in the early evening, I see maybe thirty, forty people gathering up on the bridge. Then all at once they scatter yellow rose petals into the water, and as the river carries them past the café it is as though there was a reflection in the water of the cloths of heaven.

Music is invisible movement.

Nancy Huston, *Fault Lines*

Playing for the funeral of the young pizza maker, accompanying Laure as she accompanied his mother through this terrible experience, activated something for me. It was like switching an item of clothing from the dressing-up box to the wardrobe. Music began to reinfuse my daily life.

Our piano was an antique, parallel-strung Erard, the make Chopin used to play on. We'd bought it from a piano restorer in Paris who had his *atelier* in the corner of a multi-storey car park in the 18th arrondissement and a family home in our region. He was passionate about early pianos and about Simone Weil. I think it was his interest in Simone Weil that commended him, and his piano, to me. The instrument we bought required so much compensation in the playing that I regretted it almost immediately – yet clung to it. It was beautiful to look at and to sit at, and in spring and summer I could play with the door into the rose garden open. It was quite a simple thing, but to have the instrument, and the garden with the roses, and the music and the leisure and the skill required, felt like an advanced degree of luxury; and I can see why some people think classical music is the domain of the snobbish few.

The Erard was very cheap, because no one wants a grand piano any more: they're too cumbersome and often difficult to play. The roses cost nothing but the time it took to prune them in the spring and dead-head them in the summer. The house was a luxury, of course, as was the time spent not in an office but at home, making music – though I taught many hours a week in the *école de musique*. But then our house too cost less, much less, than the two-bedroom flat we'd had in an unfashionable part of London. I think it is sometimes more possible than you think to make your own life. But nothing is assured. Clara says: 'When I'm grown-up, I want to live in Scotland in a stone house by a loch. Or in Siena. I can't decide.' Perhaps she will actually choose to live in Manchester, or Brighton, or even not have a choice, like many people; but I do think it is the sign of a free spirit, to persist in thinking one might choose where and how to live. Already we are well acquainted with the angel who passes through the room each time she says, 'When I'm grown-up.' It's an exercise they do at the hospital, it must be part of some protocol. They ask children with her condition what they want to be when they grow up. They do it to make the point to the child and the family that children with CF do survive into adulthood these days.

Music is a wonderful means of making friends in a new place, and where there is already an affinity it can add a unique empathy to a relationship; but not all musical friendships work, and sometimes I have found myself more committed than felt comfortable, sharing moments of intensity with people I would have avoided in a different context, and who would possibly rather have avoided me.

Of the many people who came to the house to sing or play instruments, Laure was the most puzzling. You'd say, 'We visited a lovely house on Sunday. Some friends of ours have just moved in,' and describe where it was, and she'd say, 'Ugh, that horrible place with the concrete outhouse, they must have more money than taste.' Then you'd find out that she'd tried to buy it herself but the vendors wouldn't reduce the price. Before I was five, we often visited my grandparents at weekends, driving from Preston to Lytham St Annes in a Morris Oxford. Just at the end of the journey there was a hill, and beyond it the sea. For many years, until life broadened out a bit, I believed that over *every* hill there was sea. Each time there wasn't, I was confounded. Next time, I'd think, there will be the sea. With Laure, I knew that she had the capacity for kindness and fun; I had seen it, I knew it was there. On the many occasions when I met with brittle dismissal and a careless shrug, I'd think, Yes, but next time she'll smile and I'll remember why I like her so much. It is not an approach to friendship I would recommend to my daughters.

Laure ran a small bookshop in a town upriver. It was no bigger than a single room, really, so that only one person could fit in comfortably at a time. You entered her shop with the feeling you might have had if you were going for a tarot reading or an assignation. She had read every single item in her stock, and a whole lot more besides that never got past the selection stage. People would believe themselves to be browsing quietly, unobserved, when she would suddenly appear from behind her curtain, removing her glasses. 'Not that one,' she'd say, taking the book you'd been considering and replacing it where you'd found it. 'This one first. You don't know her? This, then. *Then* that.' It was your whole education she was taking in hand, not just what you might buy to read on a train. She sold no notebooks or bookmarks. When Voltaire's *Treatise on Tolerance* became a bestseller after the *Charlie Hebdo* murders, she refused to stock it – an opportunistic piece of publishing, gift-wrapping, she called it. Yet somehow she made money. People deferred to her meekly, as they might have done to an experienced hairdresser. You didn't necessarily come out with what you wanted or had imagined, but she had a job to do, and she'd be the judge of whether it had been done well.

She was married, *en deuxième noces*, to a nice man with a beard which he stroked during the pauses between his sentences. Although she was an attractive woman, her second marriage, once her children were grown-up, seemed to cast her into a recovered *demoiselle*dom that was sometimes painful to behold. During the day she dispensed bookish wisdom and cultivated the reading habits of generations. If any of her customers had acquired an e-reader she would surely have got to hear of it and been round knocking on their door with a basket of bound volumes: 'Try this one. One of my favourites. Taste and see.' Come seven o'clock, she freshened her lipstick, picked up her basket and slipped off down the lanes to a tiny house built into the walls, with a tiny door, where her husband would cook her supper and massage her feet.

When she heard that a pianist had arrived in the village where her parents lived, she turned up at our front door with her music in a basket, in a black coat, with cherry lipstick and a well-pinned chignon. Underneath she was wearing washed-out jeans and a jumper. She was someone who was often well dressed for several different occasions at once.

Often when Laure sang it sent shivers through me, all that barbed sweetness and the clenched smile. She couldn't count or read music. That, she said, was for people who had been to a conservatoire. In Britain many amateur musicians who have come up through the grades system without ever going anywhere near a conservatoire can sight-sing and improvise harmonies perfectly. French music-making is either top-notch or at the level of primary school; skilled amateurs are rarely found. One of the most nerve-racking musical experiences of my life – and there have been a few – was accompanying Laure singing 'I attempt from love's sickness to fly' by Purcell, particularly in concerts, when I would be racing to catch up, skipping notes, hurdling whole bars to keep abreast of her. In rehearsal I'd say, 'Let's go back to that *do*, the upbeat to bar thirty-two,' and she'd stamp her foot and say, '*Do*, what *do*? I don't know *do*, don't know *re*, don't know *mi*, just sing me the phrase!' When she sang '*O mio babbino caro*', scenes from horror movies flashed past my eyes. But when she sang the *chansons auteur* of the 1960s, plangent, sour, ironic, Brecht-with-eyeliner songs, she was perfect.

For performances she dressed with complete sobriety, in long black skirts because she hated her legs, and long-sleeved blouses because she hated her arms. She loved to look at her own face in a pocket mirror. She was great in close-up, seen in parts. To say that at a distance she looked too much like what she was would be the kind of thing she might say herself. Though not *of* herself, obviously. I played for her in various venues, in churches, schools, markets, festivals, or late at night in a bar full of satirical cartoonists on a conference (only in France . . .), and it was the demureness of her performance, the total absence of vamp, that often turned it into something slyly pornographic and undeniably brilliant.

In complete contrast, there was Constance, who was as generous as Laure was clenched and grudging, a good musician with a lovely warm, natural voice. On Sunday mornings we would dash up to the organ loft, abandoning the harmonium and the choir, and catch our breath during the *prière universelle*, and she would sing while I played on the single-manual, six-stopped organ *Ave verum corpus* or *Panis Angelicus*. She had one of the most beautiful voices I have ever heard but she never sought praise or applause; it was always for the greater glory of God, in her view, whatever she did. Her husband had a duck farm and her youngest daughter, Verity's best friend, played the cornet. We had a musical relationship which brought us both more pleasure than people usually imagine is possible outside a relationship between lovers.

We didn't agree about everything. Although she had grown up in Paris, she had lived in the village for twenty years or so and had four children go through the school, and she accepted everything that went on, the way it went on, the harshness, the endless testing and awarding of scores, the obsessive regard for the average and the punitive approach to failure, the disregard for sport, art, drama and music. I felt rather crudely aspirational beside her, innovating and putting on school plays and musical events with my Dutch friend Thera, which we all knew people would really rather not have to get their children back to school of an evening to take part in. Then the teachers finally put their collective feet down and said that music could be learned out of school hours by the children of those families willing to pay, and school was for learning lessons, primarily conjugation, spelling and mathematics.

Laure asked Constance if she would join her in an Easter performance of Pergolesi's *Stabat Mater*, which is usually sung by a soprano and a mezzo, which they were, with a small chamber orchestra, which they didn't have. They asked me to accompany them on the piano. One Saturday morning in January, the three of us met up in the drawing room of our house. There is one big advantage to playing at a grand piano, which is that you are not facing the wall. Laure stood at the end of the piano, facing me, and Constance sat curled up on the sofa to my right with a pencil in her hand. Outside in the hall, which had a slippery floor, the children were playing beanbag sledging. The *Stabat Mater* opens with thirty-two bars of introduction, then the lower voice begins, reprising the tune we have just heard, and fractionally after the mezzo's entrance the soprano comes in, fugue-like, with the same word – '*stabat*' – a note higher but following the same melodic line. It is an astonishing opening to an astonishing work, because each voice is entirely separate, as though the conceit were that neither could hear the other, and yet they blend so beautifully, in their isolation, each illuminating the other. It is a work about grief, female grief, the collective experience of aloneness, and most particularly the grief of a mother.

Stabat: she stood, was standing, the imperfect tense which permits no end, she stood and is still standing, rooted to the spot, being present to the pain of the beloved child. So much of what we fear is in the future. So much of what causes us pain is in the past. The intensity of those moments when we are entirely in the present is sometimes so great as to take away all pain, because we do not reflect upon the moments but just dwell in them. *Stabat*: she stood – she didn't collapse. For as long as he was nailed there dying she stood. I like the Latin way of putting the verb first. Always in English we put the subject pronoun first – *she* stood, *he* said, *they* saw. That the action should come first, followed by a precision as to who is doing it, seems the right way round.

Much of the poetry (written four hundred years before the music) is exquisite, and Pergolesi's music shapes and carries the poetry exquisitely too. But above all, those two words captivated me: '*stabat mater*'. It ran through our lives for three months, and our children's lives. 'Where's Mama?' 'Doing the *Stabat Mater*,' as though it were a dance, like the hokey-cokey or a jive. Doing the *Stabat Mater* – sometimes I feel I'm still doing it, that thing mothers do, standing in this moment, with all the strength it sometimes takes just to stand, and no more, not to speak, or wail, or even comfort, but just stand.

We had decided to give our single performance of the piece on the evening of Good Friday, in the church, after the service. We made a poster from an image we got off the web, by a Spanish painter, showing a grieving mother, just her face, in half-profile. There was an air of poverty about her; she was not beautiful, in fact she was plain; her face was not elongated and translucent in grief, but lumpen and a bit blotchy. Most definitely *dolorosa*. When we were looking through Google Images for something suitable, we found photographs of mothers in war zones, frenzied with grief; we found medieval and early-Renaissance images of the Madonna, her grief all expressed in the curve of the spine, the submission of the body to the weight of suffering – and it is true that sometimes suffering, particularly that which comes from witnessing another's and which involves our own at our very helplessness, tends to crush the body as much as the features. Some images were secular and others religious. That's not a distinction I really recognise, though it is a distinction at the heart of French society. To me it feels more as though the religious is the elevation of the secular, the relationship between them being more like that between poetry and prose, though an atheist wouldn't see it that way. And it doesn't matter whether you think that our notions around God and the first rank of the Holy Family (as distinct from the second and third ranks of Apostles, saints, martyrs etc., down to, or as far as, the living legions of ordinary people whose lives are illuminated by an awareness of some inner light) came first and that the secular is all that made flesh, or whether you think that religion represents the best of our selves, what man, extrapolated from, refined, projected, might become; they seem linked either way.

I can see this is a vapid way of looking at it, satisfactory to neither priest nor feminist. Kathryn Hughes has written, 'The Virgin Mary has become an empty vessel into which men and women pour the ideals and hopes they cannot quite contain within themselves.' Julia Kristeva, in her discussion of the *Stabat Mater* (1977), called for a 'new discourse on maternity', a post-Christian way of talking about motherhood. A female figure assembled by men, the Virgin Mary, whether as heavenly queen, courtly lady or *mater dolorosa*, no longer convinces, commands or consoles. I wonder how it might feel for it to be otherwise, for her to be more than an empty vessel.

If someone had been telling a joke about Constance, Laure and me, it could have gone: 'Three women walk into a church, a Christian, and atheist and an agnostic . . . ' Constance was the real thing. At the end of Mass each Sunday she would gather the children at the front of the church and they would sing:

> '*Je vous salue, Marie pleine de grâce;*
> *le Seigneur est avec vous.*
> *Vous êtes bénie entre toutes les femmes*
> *et Jésus, fruit de vos entrailles, est béni.*

Sainte Marie, Mère de Dieu,
priez pour nous pauvres pécheurs,
maintenant et à l'heure de notre mort.'

I had no doubt that Constance somehow knew Mary, Mother of God; she talked to her, petitioned her, brought her troubles to her daily, and received replies. To Constance she was role model and confidante, comforter and guide.

Laure was not a churchgoer, she didn't believe a word of it. She was a fervent secularist, rationalist and realist. She had no truck with the *Stabat Mater* really, but she couldn't let go of it. The dominance of rationality and realism mostly accounts for the low esteem in which religion, religious sensibility and, in certain respects, poetry are held in France. She gulped down the *Stabat Mater*, though, as if this was something she had been thirsting for. I felt that of the three of us she was the one who was planting herself most in Mary's shoes, suffering with her. If I could have filmed her and eliminated the sound, of the three of us she would have looked most like a woman in a state of grief passing through to ecstasy.

I'm not sure if I'm an agnostic. I think I am probably more like a believer who feels that most of the time they have walked into a play of the thing they believe in, rather than the thing itself. In the Pergolesi, the instrumental part doesn't just accompany the two voices: the relationship is triangular, and I saw my part as a kind of mediator between their two positions. I don't think I have ever seen the Virgin Mary as an empty vessel for my hopes and ideals – what would those be exactly? I think that for me, as for most of the women I knew, hopes and ideals were more the department of the Ministry for Women's Rights, even if that was a rather dingy sub-department of Health and Social Affairs. But there were moments of intense identification with this new Mary. She too had changed – by the time of the crucifixion she would have been no Giottesque virgin, more of a broad-hipped matron with rough hands and back pain. Just as I read Emma Bovary differently (and more tolerantly) thirty years on from when I first met her, so I read Mary quite differently as a mother to how I might have as a teenage girl. There is a Mary for all seasons: *mater virgo* (the young mother), *mater speciosa* (the mother made lovely by her rapture at the crib) and *mater dolorosa*, the grieving mother. Colm Tóibín, in *The Testament of Mary*, even imagines a fugitive Mary who did not stay until the moment of death and hold her son's body in her arms but left others to bury him and fled to save her own skin. Most of the time we have no need of icons, but no mother would deny all acquaintance with the *mater dolorosa*. The grieving mother is perhaps a less obvious icon for our age than for the one in which she first appeared, the time of the Black Death, but she still walks through our days and years, passing, repassing, stepping round us, colliding with us. In these fleeting moments of identification, when the fit is, for an instant, perfect, she is less a vessel than an instrument, through which we sound our outrage and pity, self- or otherwise.

For the performance we provided a French translation of the Latin text, but the music is sufficiently expressive; it translates the text by itself. The narration starts with her in the third person, close up, then moves out to relate her grief to the grief of the world, then the narrator-singer addresses the virgin mother, mingling grief, hers and ours, then asking for her support on Judgement Day, and finally addressing Christ: 'While my body here decays,/May my soul Thy goodness praise,/Safe in paradise with Thee.' A gradual disembodiment takes place during the singing of the work. Music guides the interplay between first and third persons. The work seems to move from the mortal to the immortal, from the individual instance to the universal. As the work progresses the harmony deepens, grows rounder; the plaintive melodic lines thicken up from maiden to matron. After all, Mary did bear lots of other children.

Julia Kristeva describes a stage in an infant's development when it passes from the 'semiotic' (an emotional field, tied to the instincts, associated with the musical, the poetic, the rhythmic and that which lacks structure and meaning; closely tied to the feminine) to the 'symbolic' (the space in which the development of language allows the child to become a 'speaking subject' and to develop a sense of identity separate from the mother). Was it possible that as my mother was dying I was experiencing this transition as an adult, aided by the experience of our work on the piece and our performance of it? I certainly experienced our *Stabat Mater* as a passing between these two fields; it became a key for me.

I stepped through the door it opened, into a world of greater possibility and resolve. Perhaps I was particularly susceptible to its cadences and harmonies and plaintive melodic lines because I knew Pergolesi was dying of tuberculosis when he wrote it. But the pathos of the death touched me less than the strength of the mother figure. It mattered that it was Good Friday, that we weren't being paid, that we were raising money for SOS Villages. That year was the year of the earthquake in Haiti and the money was sent there. It mattered that we had chosen to do this rather difficult (for us) thing for the sake of the beauty of the music and to put those who came to hear it in the same position as we were putting ourselves, at the foot of a cross. Music is a great translator from third to first person. 'She' becomes 'I' and 'I' becomes 'we'.

All art, in so far as it is simulation, takes place in the mode of metaphor. But metaphors are not mere mechanisms for pretence or make-believe. There is something magical in the connection; when we learn in school that a simile says we are 'like' something and a metaphor says we '*are*' something, the leap from simile to metaphor is the leap of faith, as well as the step taken by the child who tilts her chin and says, 'I AM Morgan le Fay,' or 'I AM a butterfly.' The great *I am*, when to anyone looking on it is quite clear that *I am not*, is a powerful affirmation. It is not quite like the *I am* I encountered in the park as a child, when a woman stepped out from inside a rhododendron bush as I was making my way down towards the lake and said, 'Do you know who I am?' and, stooping down, said low and confidentially, 'Joan of Arc!' It is not a delusion but a kind of rapturous claim, that here inside of me I can be anyone I choose. Not 'make-believe' or 'pretend to be', but actually be. Nor even 'I can be whatever I want to be,' which is much more a cry of entitlement; but 'I *am*'. During the long present moment of the *Stabat Mater*, all forty-two minutes of it, the music suspends the difference, created over the ages, between us and the mother at the foot of the cross.

Le piano que baise une main frêle
Luit dans le soir rose et gris vaguement,
Tandis qu'un très léger bruit d'aile
Un air bien vieux, bien faible et bien charmant
Rôde discret, épeuré quasiment,
Par le boudoir longtemps parfumé d'Elle.

Qu'est-ce que c'est que ce berceau soudain
Qui lentement dorlote mon pauvre être?
Que voudrais-tu de moi, doux Chant badin?
Qu'as-tu voulu, fin refrain incertain
Qui vas tantôt mourir vers la fenêtre
Ouverte un peu sur le petit jardin?

Paul Verlaine, 'Le Piano que Baise une Main Frêle'

The piano kissed by frail fingers gleams
In twilight's pink and grey shades scarce outlined,
While a sound that light as a wingbeat seems,
An air so ancient, soft and so refined
Roams cautious and as if to fear inclined
Through rooms which Her sweet fragrance long
     redeems.

What is this sudden rocking at my side,
Caressing my poor body through its pain?
Soft playful song, what might you want besides?
Unsure and slight refrain, what have you tried,
Awaiting death beside the window pane
Half open on to garden flowers outside?

One Saturday I left the house in an early-morning mist and walked over to the music school, an unattractive early-nineteenth-century house which had been bought by the municipality a decade earlier, and only scantily adapted to non-domestic use. It had been the ostentatious summer home of several generations of a prosperous Parisian family, who had made their fortune in the 1860s by producing sewing patterns for the new home seamstress on her Singer machine. There were old piles of patterns in the scullery, where the photocopier and kettle were kept, and you could mentally run up a quick pair of cycling bloomers while drinking a glass of water between pupils. I taught in the dining room, on an upright piano pushed up against the fireplace to block out the wind, the clarinet teacher in the nursery, the guitar and drum teachers in one of the upstairs bedrooms. At your shoulder as you played, you sensed the presence of women in bustle skirts, lace at their throats, asphyxiated by marriage; of men embittered by property wrangles, of country lawyers in their too-tight after-dinner garments. While I marked the fingering into *Petites Mains* my thoughts drifted to novels by Zola: a character cursed by the blood of his ancestors (also known as genes) and destined to commit murder finally raises the knife to the woman he loves in the very room in which he first met her, over dinner, back in Chapter 1. While listening to a pupil totter through *Sonate en Sol* I found myself checking the wallpaper for splashes of blood, the carpet for thin patches where it had been scrubbed, or the floorboards for clumsily hidden bundles of paper francs.

The library in our heads follows no strict system of cataloguing. In the Warburg Institute in London, the books are organised according to a system of 'good neighbours', as they might be in our heads, so that next to the book you are looking for you will find others of related interest which in a traditional system might be in a completely different wing of the building. I had a half-formed story in my head using the opening scene of *Moderato Cantabile* by Marguerite Duras, where a gunshot is heard during a child's piano lesson. The piano teacher is trying to get the child to understand the meaning of '*moderato cantabile*'.

'I don't want to play the piano,' said the child.
    In the street, outside the building, a woman screamed. A long, desperate cry, so high and loud it broke through the sound of the sea. Then suddenly it stopped.
    'What's that?' cried the child.
    'Something's happened,' the lady said.

Or a pupil might be playing Debussy and I would drift off to think of Verlaine, one-time resident of Stickney, Lincolnshire, where he taught in the village school. The poet is listening to a woman playing the piano, something melodious, slight, ephemeral. There is an open window, mention of a garden. It is a blatantly erotic poem about the provocation of desire, a bourgeois poem, an interior, a fragile young lady, a piano, etc. The sense the poet has of being rocked in a cradle ends in a small shudder. But once, googling the poem to remember the second line, I came across a desperate appeal by a French *lycéen* for help in construing it.

> Help! Homework is to write a plan for a commentary.
>
> We've just done lyricism in poetry, so I suppose we're meant to write about that, but I'm not sure. It's to do with the poet's voice, the way the poet is a being set apart from others (see Orpheus myth). I don't know what to say about it, what angle to take. In class we always seemed to end up saying it was somehow universal.

The frank hopelessness of this appeal reminded me so vividly of how inept analysis of a poem can lead you, in your desperation to 'do well', to an interpretation that has absolutely nothing to do with what the poet is – often quite simply – saying. How awful you would feel, as a teacher, knowing you had effectively obscured the poetry of both the words and the emotions from a young mind. Now the poem seems irritatingly limp to me, though I can see how a piano-playing teenager like myself who imagined, *pace* Papa, that every boy in a state of semi-arousal was terminally in love with her, might have found it moving. Universal, even, if you think the universe revolves around you.

When I got there this Saturday morning I found I had forgotten my notebook and pencil. My first pupil had arrived and was waiting for me, propped up against her motor bike, insulting her boyfriend on the phone. '*T'es con, mais vraiment. Tu m'énerves. Fous-moi la paix.*' When she saw me she quickly cut him off. Somewhere the boyfriend rolled over in bed and wondered whether it was all worth it. My phone rang. It was

Nico. 'You've left your notebook on the kitchen table. I'll bring it over. But there's something—'

'What?'

'The home rang. They say your mother's taken a turn for the worse.'

I first got engaged in my mid-twenties, and I remember saying to my fiancé the following day, 'When our parents die we will be the people who comfort each other.' It had not turned out to be the case. But it is an important part to play in another person's life. Nico cycled over, skidding on the gravel outside. He said my father was with her. My brother was on his way. 'Do you want to try and get there? I'll go and check the flights.'

But Laure had asked me to play while she sang for her friend's wedding that afternoon. It was somewhere over in the north of the *département*.

'Even if you cancelled the wedding I don't think you'd make it,' Nico said. He was almost crying. Often he was close to tears. He always stopped speaking when it happened. He stopped his tears, but you knew by his silence. His eyes turned violet.

Margot was playing the adagio from Beethoven's *Pathétique* sonata. She hadn't slept much and was jittery because of the row with her boyfriend. It didn't look as though he would be around at many crucial moments in her adult life. She made a false start. I said, 'Just take it again, from the beginning. Remember to breathe, just as though you were singing it. Here, all this line, that's one breath.' I drew a swooping line with a pencil. 'You use your fourth and fifth fingers to sing the line.' She took her breath. She banished the boy and his bedclothes and the tight, airless room where they had spent the night. While she played I stood at the far end of the room, looking out of the window at the river. A woman and two men were putting boats in the water. 'When you get to the *forte*,' I said, 'it is loud not because it is loud, but because you are very close to the source of the sound. When it goes down to the *pianissimo*, you have moved away. It is not to do with the strength of the sound being made, but how close you imagine you are to it.' She played it again, and the *pianissimo* sounded distant and faint, as though the music were being heard from very far away. My mother lay dying. Later my brother told me it was like a labour: it reminded him of his wife and childbirth. The day before, she had even taken food and water, in preparation, though surely she could not have known.

After the morning lessons I went back to the house. I took her diary from the drawer in my desk. I wanted to see something of her, and her handwriting was the closest thing, closer even than a photograph. I packed the diary along with the music for the wedding. The people getting married were not people I knew. I drove up the hill and collected Laure from her little Hansel and Gretel cottage. In the car we talked about Antoine, a roofer, who had recently taken up singing. He had gone for a lesson with Laure's teacher and walked out after five minutes. 'You know how he is.' I had played for him many times; he was a showman. Every song was a white rabbit, a conjuring trick. People sometimes applauded in the middle, as though he was ice-skating and had performed a particularly tricky turn. He should have been a travelling singer, like a travelling player, and never have gone near a concert hall. Sometimes he would take a piece of drainpipe and sing down it so you could hear it all over the village. The Mayor's cleaner, a Portuguese woman who grew vegetables in a plot down by the river, said his voice came bubbling out of her garden tap when she turned it on one evening, as though she'd turned on the radio. The priest said the chalices in the sacristy shivered when he sang his scales. He began to learn Italian from a tape he had in his van. When my children slept over at his house with his children he would drive them to school the following morning and they'd all be singing in the back of the van, in the dark, with his tools slamming about around their feet.

My phone rang. I stopped the car. Laure glanced at her watch. I had told her my mother was dying, that I was returning the following morning. She was shocked: 'Not today?' 'There are no flights today,' I said. 'You don't have to convince me.' I didn't know how to interpret that. Did she mean 'Be it on your own conscience if you don't go'? Or 'Who am I to doubt you – I know you'll do what's right'? Just when I might have taken offence at her tone, she would add a pinch of something warm, spicy and scented, and I would look at her and think, Did she mean it to sound like that? Am I just imagining it?

Sometimes during phone calls people close their eyes. I stood with my back to the car so I could only see the hills and the skyline. The countryside, this small portion of the vast openness of France, was dark green and shadowed that afternoon, with no special pockets of light; the blinds were down, the castles and the farmhouses on the hill ridges were just stones made into buildings, and without the light you could not read them for stories. My brother said they were putting my mother on what was called an 'end-of-life plan'. I suppose he was ringing for my consent, though I don't think they needed it. Morphine was involved. Yes, yes, I said. At the wedding Laure sang 'Quia Respexit' from Bach's *Magnificat*:

'For he hath regarded the lowliness of his handmaiden'. The wedding was the usual good taste/bad taste affair. The brides always seemed so sassy and slick. You expected them to whip out their iPhones in the middle of the service to scroll down a list of old lovers who might have said their vows better. I seem to enjoy playing for funerals more than for weddings, on the whole. The protagonists don't have quite the same catwalk approach. Though the undertaker, the following week, sitting perched on my father's sofa with his hands on his knees, would ask me whether I wanted my mother's face to be made up before the service. And did I have a favourite dress she might – I might like her – well, to put on . . . her? Though I should bear in mind that the body was rather twisted, it might be best just to have a gown. And had I given any thought to the colour of the silk for the lining? No, I said, really I hadn't. Well, he said, if I can just suggest, just a suggestion mind you, lilac's a lovely colour for a lady.

And music is more important at funerals than weddings. At weddings people don't usually listen much, they just want to get on with the show. But at a funeral you really feel the music is doing something nothing else can do. It is taking up time, above all else. It lasts several minutes. Several minutes more with the person you loved, in contemplation. Music gives a moment's pause. The Quakers do this with silence. I suppose it is a further refinement still.

I drove home alone: Laure had stayed for the reception. I stopped on the brow of a hill, with a green view of hills and houses and dips and rises, and castles and trees, and a low sky, though the landscape itself was raised high, like something being held aloft on a tray. I rang my cousin, so she could tell her father his sister was dying.

I do believe we can accompany people in our thoughts, and I do believe it makes a difference when we do. It is quite difficult to put other thoughts aside and be with a person in something resembling prayer. It is something I was taught as a child. In the Protestant Church you talk directly to God; you say, 'Be with my mother, give her peace, let her know I am with her, that I am standing on the brow of this hill, looking out, and that in this moment all my love is focused on her.' It is a peculiar thing to do, I suppose. In the Catholic Church I think you would normally ask the Virgin Mary and one or more saints. I find that even more peculiar, and certainly more difficult. Having said that, lately I have come to think that it is the very artificiality, the very obvious way in which the Catholic Church is full of made-up things and made-up people, relying on our believing a hundred and one impossible things before breakfast, that makes it sensible. It's the halfway-houseness, the semi-grown-upness, the setting aside of childish things, of the Protestant Church that makes me now want to pick all sorts of holes in it. It irritates in the way Shakespeare set in shopping malls or airports irritates. If we had been going to say that, we would not have started from here.

Back home, at the burnt-out end of a smoky afternoon, the children were making a fairy ring on the scrap land by the river, the freckle-faced daughter of the singing roofer, my two daughters and the little black dog. They were wearing velvet capes with satin linings and making signs with sticks and invoking spirits. Nico and I went to the church and lit a candle. I said to my mother, 'Hold on till I get there.' Antoine came to fetch his daughter after tea and I handed him back a folder of music. I had been supposed to accompany him in a concert in a small chapel in the hills the following weekend. He had been practising for months. 'But surely,' he said, 'by then—'

'I don't know,' I said. 'I can't be sure.'

He took the music and went off to try and find someone else. After the children were in bed I wrote an email to a friend in the village and said that I had been in the church and had said 'Hold on till I get there.' I wrote: 'But actually I should have said, "It's OK, if you want to go, you don't have to wait for me."' When the phone rang fifteen minutes later and my father said, 'She died a quarter of an hour ago,' I felt my words had untied the painter and let her loose.

Three months later Miss Jourdain came to stay
with me, and on Sunday, 10th November, 1901,
we returned to the subject [of their visions at
Versailles], and I said, 'If we had known that a
lady was sitting so near us sketching, it would
have made all the difference, for we should have
asked the way.' She replied that she had seen no
lady. I reminded her of the person sitting under
the terrace; but Miss Jourdain declared that there
was no one there.

C. A. E. Moberly and E. F. Jourdain, *An Adventure*

Often, in September, my mother would pack up a picnic – not much of a picnic, no great splendour: sandwiches, chocolate biscuits, apples, sometimes fairy cakes contributed by my grandmother from a sponge mix out of a packet (back in the 1970s, when for a brief spell a woman's time felt too valuable to spend it making cupcakes). We'd sit out in the car on the drive while my father lingered in the house, twiddling with the radio aerial to try to get the football results as they came in. This was before car radios, even. In my memory this is something that happened every late summer – afternoon teas and lazy games of cricket in the park; not just any park but a vast estate made of meadows, ornamental driveways, a gazebo set back in the trees by a lake, a picturesque bridge, thickets and rhododendrons and the edge of Sherwood Forest, heathland where the ball got lost in long, dry, end-of-summer grasses. But in fact they cannot have happened very often. Only in September, really, would the weather and the light have been right. And every second Saturday my brother and my father would have been at 'the match' in Sheffield, mysteriously folded into the dark-clothed crowd of men that flooded down the hill to the ground, and then, buoyant or disconsolate, surged back the other way after the final whistle. So that only leaves two Saturdays in each September, over a period of maybe seven years, on many of which it must have rained. But there it sits in my memory, sure of its place, so it must have happened, at least once.

Sometimes, if his team had lost at the away match, my father would be grim-faced. They'd have appointed a new manager over the summer, and it was already clear it was not going to be good, he'd squandered money on a flashy player to draw a crowd. My grandmother, squeezed up against me in the back of the car, her tan pop-socks held up by the rubber bands the postman dropped in the driveway, refusing to go in the powder-blue Anglia with my grandfather because he strayed from one side of the road to the other, would observe that a fool and his money were easily parted. To get to the park we had to drive through the village where we 'worshipped' on Sunday mornings, in the ugly red-brick Methodist chapel beyond the flying-station. As we passed it, she would set her lips in disapproval. Even the disrespect she felt for church-going was grudging. My parents would drop in to see her after church and she'd observe, sliding an eye at the clock: 'They didn't keep you long, then?'

Back then the National Trust image had not quite been burnished and polished to the bright shine it has today; the heritage atmosphere was not quite *au point*. My mother 'served' on the committee of the local branch of the Save the Children Fund, alongside a certain Lady Scarborough who occasionally opened her house to the public. And Princess Alexandra had come to the art college where my uncle worked to declare some aspect of it open. That was as close as we came to anything grand. Everything else was history – kings, queens, ancient buildings, books. But as we drove into Clumber Park on Saturday evenings, I had a sense of stepping into an enchanted world where, because history ruled, anything could happen, time being not quite itself. Somehow key to this sense was the fact that the great house by the lake had burned down in the 1930s. This became entangled in my mind, when I was around ten, with the plot of my favourite novel, *The Amazing Mr Blunden*, so that the park came to stand for the whole idea of fiction: here things could happen that did not appear to happen in the world; ghosts might appear to you by the lake and beg for help, you might gather herbs for a potion, or go back in time to redeem characters who had done wrong. It was a powerful mix. My abandoned novel that includes the scene with the riddle in church as well as the man whistling the Bach cantata in the New World included an evocation of this place, into which I sewed possibilities for development in a number of different directions.

In the draft, the Fletcher family – a doctor, his wife and daughter Francesca – are driving from Sunday-morning church in a Methodist chapel to the annual church picnic, at harvest time, when the car runs into a cloud of smoke drifting across the road from a burning stubble field. Out of the smoke appears a woman, holding her young daughter, about Francesca's age, by the hand. The child is having difficulty breathing. The mother asks if they can sit in the car for a few minutes. The family deposit her a little further on, once the smoke is clear. When the picnic has been laid out and they are about to eat, the Reverend Bernadino, the visiting African minister, says grace. And because Francesca doesn't close her eyes, because she keeps them open just when you are supposed to shut them, she sees the mother and daughter again, and it is clear to her at that moment that they are ghosts. I stalled because I couldn't get them past the picnic and down to the lakeside. I know who all these people are, their backgrounds, their secrets. How do things move forward? We suffer and stagnate, I read recently, because we are not prepared to give up something about ourselves, some fond illusion or festering resentment. I am hovering up by the rhododendrons for fear of going down to the lake. What is it I fear I might find there? I have convinced myself that the story can never be continued or completed, that the moment at which it stops is a moment beyond which I may not go. Of such threads and patches is every attempted writing career made. I have been trying to get down to the lake for so many years. Almost as long as I have been trying to catch hold of the elusive cloud of balloons I saw on my first day in Paris.

After the fire only a few buildings remained – stables and greenhouses, the estate workers' cottages and an overgrown kitchen garden. There was a kind of imprint of the house where it no longer stood, in people's minds. At nearby Roche Abbey you can still see the ground plan of the twelfth-century monastery, but at Clumber the past is more of a shadow on the grass. The surviving buildings have all been restored now, but back then everything was overgrown. There were gates which might have led somewhere, which you didn't quite dare go through. I thought that down by the lake, like the two academic ladies who visited Versailles in the 1900s and walked through the gardens and saw Marie Antoinette, I might go back in time; but even in real life we never went to the lake. On the outer fringe of the park, where we pic-nicked, people walked their dogs, grand-looking ladies in headscarves, huge bottoms in tweed skirts. For some reason I thought they had all escaped from the mental asylum on the other side of Sherwood Forest, the one where I'd met Joan of Arc, an Edwardian house of some splendour. Women of my own mother's age were sent there for giving no greater sign of insanity than having a child out of wedlock. My father used to go there to visit Auntie Edie, who was said to have lost her mind when her son died at the age of twelve, of scarlet fever. Her mind gave way, like a bridge or a building under too much weight, and she wandered the grounds of the hospital muttering, 'No money, no clothes, no money, no clothes, no house, no money, no clothes.'

The morning after my mother died, I flew back to England, after a very early start. My brother and father were already standing in the drive of the house I'd grown up in, in dark suits, waiting for me. We went in my father's car to Clumber Park, to the café, which had not existed when we went there as children, in the former schoolmaster's house from the old days of the estate. Almost everyone who went there was old and apparently sweet-toothed. Afterwards we walked by the lake where we had never walked as children but where my parents had often come in the days of my father's retirement, before my mother became ill. I realised that the greater part, the longest part of my parents' marriage had taken place in between our leaving home and the day of her death. We laughed a bit about the way my mother would quote Robert Frost's poem: 'The Road Not Taken', and how it used to drive my father wild when she did it, in a rather portentous voice, heavy with implied meaning. She was fond of quoting poetry.

I celebrate myself, and sing myself,
And what I assume you shall assume,
For every atom belonging to me as good
    belongs to you.

Walt Whitman, Leaves of Grass

During the long week between my mother's death and the funeral I flew back to France to play in Antoine's concert. I drove listening to Tchaikovsky's *'Octobre: Chant d'Automne'* on the radio. It was a time of year when my mother was happiest, in her garden, which she preferred to the house. Suddenly I remembered returning from school with a stiff new leather satchel and unspoiled exercise books, coming into the back garden to find her raking the soil, having stripped out the tomato plants, and setting the green tomatoes aside for wrapping in newspaper later on. She looked up and smiled, and no doubt asked how my day had been. It was not a carefree smile, more a careless one, as though she had many more of the same, that this was by no means precious or rare, which is how you like your mother to smile when you are young. Later she'd make the ripe tomatoes into soup.

The Methodist minister had been to visit us. He was to conduct my mother's funeral service, but, since he had not known her, had come to ask us about her so he could prepare his eulogy. The minister looked at me rather sharply as my father showed him out after our chat, in which each of us appeared to have described a quite different person to him, and said, like a police constable, 'If you remember anything else, just let me know.' My father spoke of her sense of duty, her simple Christian faith, her strong discipline as a teacher and before that as a young WRAF officer. I spoke of her love of nature poetry and the Lakes, of her garden and her wish that my brother and I be able to venture into the world unimpeded by prejudice or narrow-mindedness. My father looked surprised. It was like a weirdly personal balloon debate, each arguing for a particular version of the loved one. Each of us not only wanted our own version of the person to be kept in the balloon, we actively wanted to throw the other version out. So when I got home I sat down and wrote to the minister, while there was still time, describing how I loved to find my mother in the garden at the end of the day, absorbed and happy in what she was doing, and making soup later on. I said that I would be happy if my children remembered such things of me. At the airport that morning I had told my father that I regretted how much cause I must have given her to worry. Now, with daughters of my own, I could begin to appreciate how crippling that worry might be, how much better it would have been not to put her through it. How I could have spared her too the semi-scornful eye, the one that follows the mother of teen-age girls down the road in her not-quite-right outfit with her hair not quite right and on her way to do an insignificant thing that will not change the world. Return some library books, or visit a friend who is not exactly in need, just bored or lonely. How did life become that humdrum? thinks the teenage daughter. When did she begin to let herself go? My father said: 'Ah, but you gave her so much joy, too.' And I do remember asking her when she had been at her happiest in her life. She answered, 'When you were little, the two of you.' That seemed a sad answer at the time. I vowed that I would not have this answer to give my own daughters, that I would try to be like Pooh and say today is my favourite day, right to the end.

For the concert Antoine had hired a Steinway – top of the range, he confessed. He hadn't been able to find another pianist. Sometimes you know you shouldn't do something, that you will do it badly, that people will be irritated by you doing it badly, that you will wish you hadn't done it, but just at the moment when you should be saying no, you don't have the energy. I knew a man who decided one 31 December that every morning from now on he would get up and look at himself in the mirror and practise saying, 'No.' On 1 January his girlfriend walked into the bathroom and found him saying, 'I'm terribly sorry . . . um . . . I'm afraid I just . . . can't . . . ' His girlfriend said that was ridiculous, he just had to say no.. It seemed odd that he should say it to himself in the mirror instead of to an imaginary other.

I didn't say no. A young woman from the village who looked like a French Mia Farrow was due to sing in the concert alongside the roofer, Purcell mostly. But she also wanted to sing Fauré's *Pie Jesu*.

'No, really,' I said, 'I don't think . . . '

'Please?'

'OK.'

I found myself crying as I played for her. It didn't matter that I couldn't read the music in front of me – my fingers found their own way, I'd played it so often, for exam students, choristers, divas, in church, in village halls. Everyone loves to sing '*Dona eis requiem*'. I'd been moved many times before by this music, by a child treble touching the highest notes, by the smooth shifts in the harmonies, cradling the pale, lonely voice, but this time it was because of that plural *eis*, as I saw my mother joining the millions and millions who had gone before her, being granted rest. I notice that the

USB key that is saving these files as I write is the one they gave me afterwards with the recording of the recital, which I have never listened to.

But I wanted to play at my mother's funeral. 'She would have liked', 'she would have said', 'she would have . . . ' slipped into our sentences for the first time in our lives. The minister said to me, 'Make me a sign if you are OK to play.' I made a sign that was meant to say OK, but which he interpreted as 'not OK', so then I had to sort of put my hand up and wave it around to get his attention and it felt like being at primary school. I played on a black upright piano on which I had accompanied the Sunday school when I was a young teenager and beginning to find any participation in compulsory church services that wasn't strictly musical quite agonising. The piano and organ have the advantage that you almost always play with your back or profile to the public. When I went with my father to the church the evening before the funeral to check the piano was in tune, I played the piece through while he waited. The order of service was laid face-down in every seat in the church, pew after pew. We had persuaded my father to accept printing a pretty photograph of my mother, from perhaps her seventies, where she looked radiantly happy, on the back of the service sheet. He had expressed a wish for something 'more formal', which we had coaxed him out of, especially when it turned out that what he favoured was her last passport photo. Now we could see maybe 150 identical images of my mother laid out, place after place, smiling gently. My father said as we left the church that the thing he found most difficult wasn't that, but seeing the trestles left out for the coffin to be placed on the following day.

Twice in the car following the hearse my father asked which way her head was, this or that. I was pretty sure the head was at the driver end. The funeral director, straight out of George Eliot, walked down the road in front of the hearse and a man who was cutting the hedge of the house next door removed his cap and stood with it clutched to his chest as the procession went by. During the funeral I stood with my brother and father in the front pew and my husband and children were behind to my right. At one point during a hymn I looked over my shoulder and saw Nico violet-eyed, biting his lip, and Verity holding tight to his hand, looking exactly like a child holding on tight to a helium balloon, anchoring him. In the crematorium they played the slow movement of the Mozart clarinet quintet as the coffin came in; and after it had left, behind the curtain, 'Morning' from the *Peer Gynt* suite. At the awful moment when the curtains close and you know that the beloved body, the body that gave birth to you, is being incinerated, I did not quite realise it was already happening because the minister was intoning, 'Ashes to ashes, dust to dust,' and I was thinking how the words and his way of saying them would have pleased her.

We chose 'Morning' for a holiday we had had in Norway when I was seven and my brother nine, when the skies were constantly fresh and blue, though we did not get to visit Grieg's house because it was closed on Thursdays. And we chose the Mozart because we remembered her playing it, accompanying each of us on the piano for our clarinet exams. In the kitchen when people were having tea and coffee a woman who had lost her own mother recently and was in her fifties and wearing a Conservative Party Conference-type suit said to me, 'Did you see the butterfly, Helen? Up in the roof of the church?' I had seen it. To another of her friends I said, 'Dorothy, she really loved you,' and she, a terribly frail, pretty woman, undergoing radiotherapy at the time, turned her meek eyes upon me and said with extraordinary emphasis, as though her voice would break under the force of the sentiment it carried, 'And I loved her too.'

If I could write like Jane Kenyon, if I could write poetry at all, I would not need to write these thousands of words. I would take a sieve, or a riddle, as my mother called it – the one she shook the sandy soil of her garden through, for our house stood on the site of a former quarry and the soil was almost like a beach – and shake it till the small things had sifted through, and only the substantial, perhaps misshapen but significant, pieces remained, and there would be my poems.

> Let the light of late afternoon
> shine through chinks in the barn, moving
> up the bales as the sun moves down.
>
> Let the cricket take up chafing
> as a woman takcs up her needles
> and her yarn. Let evening come.
>
> Let dew collect on the hoe abandoned
> in long grass. Let the stars appear
> and the moon disclose her silver horn.
>
> Let the fox go back to its sandy den.
> Let the wind die down. Let the shed
> go black inside. Let evening come.

To the bottle in the ditch, to the scoop
in the oats, to air in the lung
let evening come.

Let it come, as it will, and don't
be afraid. God does not leave us
comfortless, so let evening come.

Jane Kenyon, 'Let Evening Come'

PART TWO

Moving Back

Ideally, what should be said to every child, repeatedly, throughout his or her school life is something like this: 'You are in the process of being indoctrinated. We have not yet evolved a system of education that is not a system of indoctrination. We are sorry, but it is the best we can do. What you are being taught here is an amalgam of current prejudice and the choices of this particular culture. The slightest look at history will show how impermanent these must be. You are being taught by people who have been able to accommodate themselves to a regime of thought laid down by their predecessors. It is a self-perpetuating system. Those of you who are more robust and individual than others will be encouraged to leave and find ways of educating yourself – educating your own judgements. Those that stay must remember, always, and all the time, that they are being moulded and patterned to fit into the narrow and particular needs of this particular society.

Doris Lessing, *The Golden Notebook*

The children started in the local school aged three and six. Clara had been in a primary school in London, and Verity had been in a nursery, the kind where you learn to weave baskets from willows grown in the garden, which until a recent makeover by the council was a car park. We were not keen on private schooling, and felt glad that our children were going to enter the French system, where they would benefit from *liberté*, *égalité* and *fraternité* and learning conjugation.

'*C'est une grande famille,*' the headmaster assured us. After the primary school in Kentish Town – multicultural, politically correct, child-centred, with so many authors coming to read to the children, so many chess champions queuing up to teach them their times tables and future Olympic athletes teaching them to pole-vault and shoot ball that you sometimes couldn't cut a path to your child's coat peg – it seemed delightfully uncluttered.

The school was built to a Napoleonic plan. There was a hazelnut tree, and the children gathered nuts and ate them at break. They sat at desks in pairs. They called the teachers '*maîtresse*' and '*maître*' and did dictation. They wrote out calculations and spellings on slates and waved them in the air. When I met a class down at the river while I was walking the dog in the afternoon, in a crocodile, they would break ranks and cluster round the dog calling, '*Poésie, Poésie!*' Our dog was called Posy, but people in the village called her Poésie. Surely they didn't think we would actually call our dog Poetry, as the baker might call his dog Baguette?

Though we made an effort over quite a few years to teach her to obey, she was an unregenerate free spirit, the last thing anyone wants in a dog. As she streaked through one of the allotment gardens by the river in pursuit of a rabbit the gardener would look up in fury, fill his lungs and furiously yell: '*Poésie!*'

Our favourite walk was 'round the gardens'. I loved it for itself, but also because the 'stepping out' aspect of it, that little perambulation you could do from the house with only ten minutes to spare before supper or school, reminded me of the brisk walks my mother and father used to do around the housing estate, arm in arm. Round the gardens was much prettier and there were no houses, but it was the nature of the walk, the spirit in which we did it, that reminded me of them. And since my mother was unable to do any of these things for herself any more, I found myself taking pleasure in doing them on her behalf. I wonder if this is part of the process of growing older. I would have been apprehensive, twenty years ago, to think I might assume some of the characteristics of my mother, and considering how things went for her it is not all that happy a thought even now, but it is definitely the case that I found myself, and still do, doing things because she did them. I find a comfort in doing them, and I see it brings my children the same pleasure it gave me then. When I stop to think how infuriating I found her when I was a late teenager, and even into my thirties, it bodes ill for my relationship with my own children. Ah well. Perhaps this is what people call compromise, in the way they used to tell me that relationships were 'all about compromise'. Still, it is cheering to think that I have found, in the one stable relationship I have ever had to anyone I wasn't related to by blood, with my husband, that compromise doesn't play nearly such a big role as people gleefully, gloomily predicted.

Posy's mother, a Brittany spaniel, was rescued off the street by an Englishwoman. We went to visit her compound one Sunday afternoon, shortly after we moved from London. Posy was the only black puppy; the other two were reddish, like their mother. Posy threw herself at Clara. We later read that you should probably take the puppy who doesn't do that, the one who hides in the corner; the all-guns-blazing one is likely to be a handful. We collected our handful a couple of weeks later. We were meant to wait until she had been weaned, but the mother died of a tumour before that could happen, and Posy was still only six weeks old. She was a bit bigger than a guinea pig, though not much. She cried terribly at night. She slept in a dog-training cage in our bedroom, and every time she cried Nico got out of bed, picked her up and put her in her tray or, after a week or so, out of the back door. Eventually he got her to sleep through the night, but at the time it seemed even tougher than all the sleepless nights with babies. She got a bit bigger, and had her injections, and we tried to take her for walks, but often she would just sit down in the middle of the path by the river and refuse to go any further, like an old mule, and we had to pick her up and carry her home. We tried training her – a neighbour in London recommended cheese as an inducement – but neither the best *tomme* from the cheese van on the market nor twiggy doggy meaty treats from the supermarket would induce her to do anything whatsoever to order. She wouldn't fetch a stick, or come when you called her, or walk on a lead, or stay, or sit. We saw other people walking serenely along the river path with their dogs at their heels and we wondered whether they were using black magic. Posy was amiable and seemed very happy to be part of our family, but, as they say is the case of the dogs of people who fail to train their animals properly, she clearly believed that she was one of us. People who knew about dogs would say knowingly, 'Ah, just you wait, listen to the dog and she'll train you,' and we would hang our heads and look sheepish, waiting for Posy to come and round us up and get us into the kitchen, or the laundry room where the dog food was kept. But I think she was as bad at it, for a dog, as we were as humans. As we failed to train her, so she failed to train us.

Clara loved school from the start. She made friends among the boys and was included in their games. Her sense of fun seemed to lift her into the air; she was barely earthed. Her teacher said, 'When she isn't here the class isn't the same. It's just an ordinary day.' She loved learning French. After a couple of weeks she came home electrified, her eyes alight, her little satchel bouncing on her back. 'I did it! I spoke French!'

'What did you say?'

'I said, "*Je veux du papier*"! I wanted a piece of paper so badly, the words just FLEW out!'

They continued to fly, and she was quickly fluent, experimenting, testing and squeezing the words like a good French *mère de famille* sniffing fruit and vegetables on the market, judging their sweetness and ripeness. Verity, more cautious, waited. Then one day she brought home a friend, who remained her friend, a well-rooted, serene little child. Verity had chosen well and wisely. Félicie taught her French, and how to be French.

On the evening of the first day, at five o'clock, there was an aperitif in the schoolyard. We stood around under the plane trees and the older children and teachers served drinks and small things to eat. Clara reached out for a crisp. She can't eat anything that contains fat unless she takes a pill containing pancreatic enzymes to enable her to digest the fat, and I was just feeling in my pocket for her pills when an older girl's arm shot out, grabbed Clara's hand and stopped her. '*On n'a pas le droit!*' she hissed. Nico and I looked at each other. *On n'a pas le droit* is the French for 'It's not allowed.' Literally, 'You've no right.' *J'ai le droit* was something a child would say if you asked them not to spit on the floor where there wasn't a notice actually forbidding it.

At least we understood these nuances, we spoke French – most people thought Nico actually was French. I worked at the music school, Nico helped run the rowing club and was generous with his time and skills as a mender, fixer and smoother-out of people's difficulties. He organised exhibitions in the annual summer festival. We loved France, its landscape, language, way of living; its literature – *hélas*! All this, along with the immersion in music, meant we were welcomed, invited and accepted. I never knew quite who was in the house, as there were several entrances and exits, and the local people and our friends passed casually through all the time. I was not the kind of mother who held court in the kitchen with a tea-cloth over her shoulder, so I was often quite glad to find someone else doing it for me. And it was a paradise for young children. Childhood itself is a paradise for young children, as long as we don't mess it up for them. In winter they played with dozens of other children, often up in the attic, making dens, riding the rocking horse in a frenzy across deserts, building pirate ships and improvising circuses. They foraged for walnuts and plums on the disused railway line and rode their bikes by the river, racketing over the ruts in the dry mud path. Often we cycled to a dragonfly pool, with Posy in the basket of Nico's bike. You had to cross the bridge and climb up the road on the other side, then plunge down to follow a delicious stream which ran turquoise past a water mill, leave the bikes in the grass and scramble down and cross the stream on stepping stones. The adults always flopped on the grass, mostly having lost the knack of play, and would only swim in that solemn way we have, to cool off when our lunch had 'gone down'. The children went exploring, crawling out on the bough of a tree that overhung the pool, like the tiger in *The Jungle Book*, and in summer lying along it in the sun till they were unbearably hot, then sliding off lazily into the fresh, icy water. I didn't know there were dragonflies till one day they all hatched at once, and we found ourselves walking through clouds of them, wings glistening with that newborn quality of near-wetness that catches the sunlight and makes them sparkle on the upper side, and cast miniature shadows on the water below.

Above the pool was a ruined abbey. There was a story that a young nun had become pregnant and had thrown herself off the cliff down into the pool with her baby in her arms. At least, people said it was a story, but it didn't seem to quite add up to one. It lacked a plot. How might my mother have improved on it? Perhaps the bishop's illegitimate son, the father of the child, adopted as a baby by the lord of the nearby castle, had that day married her older sister in a ceremony conducted by the bishop. The tyranny of the plot is a strange psychological phenomenon. But it's true that Nico and I have spent many hours, walking across the Mendip Hills and the Somerset Levels, saying, 'What happened?' Trying, in other words, to work out the plot.

One of my oldest friends was bringing up her four daughters elsewhere in France. Although their parents were both English, they had all four been born there. The oldest said to me when she was fourteen: 'If you want your children to grow up happy in France they must fit in. And if you want them to fit in you must never let them watch CBeebies, or read English books that you love, or teach them to sing "My Bonnie Lies Over the Ocean".' I did not take any notice of this advice. We didn't have a television, but the children watched DVDs of British shows. They also watched *Barbapapa*, from which they learned French, but for laughs they watched things in English. At the *maison de la presse* we bought a weekly magazine with a free DVD of three episodes of *Bewitched*, or *Ma Sorcière Bien Aimée* as it's called in French. Samantha, the 1950s housewife who occasionally gets round the irritations of her sequestered bourgeois existence by twitching her nose and doing a little magic, was a great hit. The local children used to pile in and watch it with the French soundtrack on, all squashed up on one sofa. And our children fitted in.

For a while – until they learned to speak French really fluently – it was assumed that the differences between them and the other children were due to the language. Paradoxically, it was once they had learned to speak French like the local children that the real differences started to show. They weren't richer or smarter or better, but they were *different*. They laughed at different things, they were more independent-minded, they made up games and disguised themselves and ran through the streets. They were popular, and children flocked to the house. It was only at the age when the disguises were dropped and the earphones went in that it suddenly became a problem, and more apparent, if you didn't blend in.

One day Clara came home and said, 'I'm the only child in the whole school who believes in fairies.' She was six, maybe seven. 'I mean,' she said, 'I don't actually believe in them, I haven't seen any, but I know what it means, I know what fairies feel like. Sometimes,' she said, loading her schoolbooks on to the kitchen table and turning to the page in her maths book for homework, 'the others think I'm babyish. But it's not that kind of believing in fairies. I just mean I believe there are some things you can't explain, or see. You can't not believe in something just because you can't see it. They can't see inside my lungs. They can't see I've got an illness, but I have.'

She had met a boy in Cornwall the previous Easter. He was probably twelve at the time. In the sand he made drawings for Clara. 'These,' he said, 'are angel wings.' He drew a body with wings at the back, attached like birds' wings. 'And these are fairies' wings. They attach at a single point — so. And what are these?' He drew more wings.

'Fairies' wings again. They're the same.'

'Right, and wrong,' the boy said. 'They're the same. But these are butterfly wings. Fairies and butterflies have exactly the same wings.'

And that, Clara said, is about the most interesting thing anyone's ever taught me.

The other day, in Somerset, I drove past a wooden sculpture by the side of the road: an angel, crouching. His wings were folded up behind him, not spread wide, and I was struck by how feathery they were. I suppose I had never given much thought to what angels' wings are made of. School nativity plays had led one to think they were made of cardboard covered with aluminium foil. But the sculptor had really emphasised the featheriness of the angel's wings, its closeness to something avian.

Clara was often an ecstatic pupil, with a considerable capacity for rapture, but on her report the teachers said things like 'inclined to daydream' and, once, 'Clara appears to know little about her own medical condition,' because she had been unable to label alveoli on a diagram. 'I think I do know,' Clara said. 'I know what it feels like. I know what it *is*.'

She decided, in advance of a class trip to the sea, to give a presentation about her illness; if it could be discussed openly, people might stop asking her questions about how many pills she took a week (129), how many hours of physio she did a week (three or four), when did she think she'd die, twenty-eight? Twenty-nine? In Britain a four-minute film had been made, with Charlie and Lola-type characters, to inform children about CF, and Clara translated it and re-recorded it in French with a friend. It took them a long time. When Clara and her friend's mother, who had done the editing, asked permission to show it, the teacher said, 'Oh, let's just download something off the internet. Don't get involved. Otherwise people will say, "Not her again!"' 'Why would they say that?' asked my Dutch friend whose son had helped Clara make the film in French. 'She's not exactly a pushy child. It's much better for her to do it herself. It's not easy to talk about a disability. Especially here.'

So Madame Moreau stood at the back of the room with her arms tightly folded while Clara stood on a chair and pulled a string hanging down from the ceiling, which unleashed a roll of brown paper that unscrolled from ceiling to floor with all the medicines on she took in one week. She was funny and brave in her presentation. The children asked to see the film a second time. They all asked questions, including the one about mortality. They were only nine then. Things were still OK. Afterwards Mme Moreau said, 'I can't think why you didn't get her to do it earlier.'

During the school trip, one of the mothers who had accompanied the class, who kept an eye on Clara and made sure she took her medicines, rang one evening and said, 'Clara is so full of joy. She loves her life. God will make it a long one.' The next day the class visited a place called the *lac noir*. The doctors had said Clara must go nowhere near stagnant water, particularly ponds, or to anywhere where the conditions were like those of a hothouse, and Clara knew this, and I had told Mme Moreau before the children left. Later I learned that a teacher had held Clara by the hand, though she was nine, and did not require or desire hand-holding, and marched her along to the black lake. Parents could be overprotective. After a while Clara wrenched her hand away, turned on her heels and ran. The mother who rang me had run with her from that dark, rank, humid place till they reached the beach and the salt water, and lay on the sand, gulping in the sea air. 'The minute you start to feel love for a child,' the woman said, 'you start breathing like them. I had a pain in my lungs like hers.'

We had been to see the headmaster before we moved and explained that Clara had cystic fibrosis, which in French is called *la mucoviscidose*. It is a word that draws attention to the fact that the sufferer's lungs and other organs fill up with sticky mucus. '*Les mucos*', they call them, a term we all found bizarre and unhelpful. At first the headmaster, a man hewn from a breezeblock with a rulebook in his back pocket, didn't seem to be quite sure he was the headmaster, until the teacher of the class for six-year-olds reminded him. 'Ah, yes,' he said, drawing up a teeny-weeny chair at a teeny-weeny desk. 'In France we know all about that illness. We had a famous pop star, you know, Gregory, he died of it, so there was a lot of publicity.' Fortunately Clara at this point knew no French, so what she didn't understand couldn't hurt her. But it set something flashing in my mind, the idea that people knew about CF because a star had died of it, very young. The man in question had won the French equivalent of *The X Factor*, and hidden the fact, amazingly, that his lungs were collapsing. He was twenty-four. A couple of years later, because he'd been used by the fund-raising organisation to publicise the condition, children would say to Clara in the playground, 'There's no point asking what you want to be when you grow up, you're going to *die* when you're twenty.' And if we put it to the teachers that it would be helpful for them to discourage the children either from seeing the illness in these terms, or from throwing this in Clara's face, since she was only eight, the teachers said, 'Yes, but this is normal. He was a celebrity.' It was as though we had been complaining that the press were at our door when we had chosen to put our child into a movie. We hadn't chosen anything. But it was understandable that children should say that. It was what their parents said, in connection with Clara. And in a way they were right, every-body was right, except those who believed that you could not teach children to be kind or to put themselves in another person's shoes.

For coping with Clara's special medical need they had a protocol. It was caring by numbers. But I never felt that any one of her five teachers ever understood or even tried to imagine what having the illness might mean, how it might feel on the inside to have it, physically, emotionally, socially. The approach was so to treat her that she would be indistinguishable from the others. That was the objective, with her and every other child. That they should learn to resemble a child who has been through the French school system, as their parents and teachers had before them. Even the rebelliousness we saw in the *lycéens* and students on the news was just another aspect of that. '*Ah, oui, c'est ça, le jeune Français, il proteste.*' But he doesn't, not really. It's just another way of following the protocol. Solidarity isn't a challenge if you're French. Tolerating difference is.

I breathed enough to take the Trick—
And now, removed from Air—
I simulate the Breath, so well—
That One, to be quite sure—

The Lungs are stirless—must descend
Among the Cunning Cells—
And touch the Pantomime—Himself.
How numb, the Bellows feels!

Emily Dickinson

If you have a child with a difficult illness like cystic fibrosis, you are never, ever relaxed. Even the silence in the night when the child is not coughing is stressful. You are waiting for it to be broken, bringing yet another visit from the nurse, more tests, more physiotherapy, more waiting for results and the prescription and administering of more of the dreaded anti-biotics, more reactions to antibiotics that set off a whole chain of new discomforts which require solutions of their own.

People are often surprised to hear that Clara has an illness, let alone a 'life-threatening' one. We don't discuss it much. We just do what has to be done every day and hope for a cure. I don't read all that many websites, I don't do all I should to fund-raise, I don't follow every up and down of research. I need to be totally on top of what is happening now, in this house, in this family, and deal with it well. If I know too much I won't be able to do that. I don't want to have too much of a sense of the plot, or of the variety of possible 'outcomes'. Either she will be OK or she won't. But of course that is wrong-headed. Many strands are woven together to make this tough, fragile, beautiful, excitable, passionate, compas-sionate, angry, brave, fearful, explosive, serene being. She is both in sickness and in health, all the time. After one more lesson on nutrition that doesn't apply to her, with instructions for healthy eating that need to be inverted for her, she comes home and says to me, 'Mummy, am I *healthy*?'

When Clara was around ten I sent away, furtively, for a book called *Parenting Children with Health Issues and Special Needs*. We had never really talked about the illness much to her, but she did her treatments, took her pills, exercised, submitted to physio, then later learned to breathe actively herself, draining her lungs 'autogenically', and knew what dangers to avoid. She had an almost primeval detector for stagnant water, where microscopic creatures breed. She was not allowed to enter greenhouses or any tropical or foetid atmosphere. We didn't refer to it as a 'life-threatening disease' or a 'life- shortening' one, as it was later more commonly known. I kept wondering if there were things I should be saying or doing that I could read about.

The book, when it arrived, advised that when a child with cystic fibrosis complains of having to do treatments instead of going out to play you should say, 'That's hard. You sound frustrated. How are you going to handle it?', but the only time I tried one of these in my own mouth the children shrank away from me as though I was talking in tongues and waving my arms around uncontrollably. Eventually Verity said cautiously, 'Err . . . have you been reading one of those self-help books again?' 'Hmm,' Clara added, hands on hips, putting her head on one side, '"And how do you think you could have handled that differently?"' Verity found the book on my desk and read out gleefully, '"When I am tired my behaviour becomes *unacceptable*"!' 'Yes!' Clara agreed, reading over her shoulder. '"I guess you could do nothing."' Then, with a menacing, narrow-eyed leer: '"But that might-not-work-out-well-for-you."'

One thing people tend to know about cystic fibrosis (or 'sixty-five roses' as it is often known, after a child who had it had difficulty, like my mother, with all those sibilant syllables) is that it requires daily physiotherapy. Just as people almost always

accompany the words 'spiral staircase' with an ascending twirl-
ing gesture, when you say 'cystic fibrosis' they often reply, 'Oh
yes, that's the one where you have to—' and then they tap their
own thorax area like a lady at the vicar's tea party with reflux.

The physio is a burden. Although it is good to feel that
exercise and conscious breathing can keep her lungs in better
condition, it is a responsibility too. Just to stay in shape, she
has to exercise every day, running and trampolining, and
then do her physio on top. She spends about as much time
doing it as other children might who were training to swim
at regional level, or to run for the county, but there are no
medals or colours, and before doing it she has to inhale saline
solution from a nebuliser that delivers a mist of salt into her
lungs. This routine enables her just to keep on top of things,
to keep just clearing the bar, as I feel I do too, just scraping
home in the time allowed, to run another day, every day.
There are many forms of disadvantage in life, and for the most
part the people who labour with them don't take it too badly.
It rankles, though, when people who have none at all accept
their well-being as a right: *j'ai le droit*.

We tapped Clara's chest, front, back and sides, for twenty
minutes daily when she was small. Her lungs at that stage were
clear, but it was a routine she and we had to learn for the day
when she would need it. We had to train her to be quiescent.
The tapper had to hold their hand in such a way that there
was a little pocket of air between their palm and the baby's
body. She didn't seem to mind. The rhythmic clapping, often
accompanied by singing, seemed to have the side-benefit of
reinforcing her sense of rhythm. To this day she has an in-built
metronome, useful for a musician.

I don't like to dwell too much on whether illness nurtures

particular character traits, though it is clear that children with conditions like CF 'do better', as they say, if they develop a measure of patience and an ability to convert their anger into more positive forms of energy. If you asked a hundred people who know Clara whether her temperament is placid or passionate, all one hundred would say passionate. The patience had to be learned.

When we moved to France, most aspects of the treatment remained the same. I had spoken beforehand to a lovely woman who had moved to a house outside a village near Toulouse. The day they bought their house, which required a lot of work and repair, she realised she was expecting a third child. When Jack was born it was quickly established that he had CF. Stephie and I talked on the telephone, I anxious about moving into the French health system, away from the NHS and Great Ormond Street, and she adamant that she could never return to England, because the treatment in France was so much better. In fact the treatment was much the same – excellent – with two differences. One was that in France we had the mobile phone number of Clara's consultant at the nearest cystic fibrosis specialist centre on speed dial and could call him at any moment. Once I called him and said, 'Clara's in the local clinic, they're just about to take her appendix out,' and he said, '*Merde*, I'm on the beach.' There are measures they use in major hospitals when operating on vulnerable patients. 'Can they helicopter her over to us?'

'I think it's a bit late.'

'OK, pass me the surgeon then.' It was nice to picture his substantial walrus frame, feet dangling off the edge of a lilo, with the Mediterranean lapping his toes, as he talked the local surgeon through the long list of special precautions.

The second difference was in the approach to physiotherapy, in that it is conducted by a professional rather than the child's parents. In England, there are physiotherapists attached to the CF centres in hospitals, and they help and advise, but the hands-on treatment every day is the responsibility of the family. Both approaches have benefits, as not every physiotherapist is a respiratory specialist, and a member of the family or the person themselves, as they get older, is probably going to be more knowledgeable and efficient. The French state paid for all of Clara's treatment, and this included five thirty-minute appointments a week. Eric, the physio in our town, was adept at treating several patients simultaneously and had a handsome fleet of vintage cars to show for it. Clara sat on a couch that went up and down at the touch of a button, while he placed his hands on her to encourage her, with pressure, to perform a sequence of breaths, then 'huffing out' with a long, sharp breath till every last bit of air was gone. You could test whether she was breathing out hard enough by holding a pocket mirror at some distance in front of her. If it steamed up she was doing it right. Over the years they designed a little obstacle course in his tiny treatment room. Between rounds of breathing Clara would stretch up and catch a bar over her head, walk with her hands along a series of rungs, leap cat-like to a shelf on the opposite wall and then back to the couch. Behind screens – close enough so that they too, had the screen not been between them, could have misted up the mirror – lay the other patients: a farmer, often, reconditioning a crushed leg, or a retired English civil servant with a shoulder injury from tennis. In the far corner a man with rheumatic fingers squeezed thoughtfully on highly sprung hand-grips. They were like a little circus gearing up for a matinée performance.

Eric's dog slept in the corner. In a dream she would stagger to her feet, then slump hopelessly back to the floor and dream further, deeper.

Eric would throw beanbags at Clara, which she had to catch as she leaped from bar to bar, and the farmer would let out a roar as he lifted his legs with weights round his ankles, like a fairground strong-man in a novel by Thomas Hardy. All this to an unchanging soundtrack of two albums, produced twenty-five years apart, and uploaded/downloaded – stuck, anyway – inside Eric's computer, which was always on 'just annoyingly audible': Norah Jones and Supertramp. The insipid flavour of the musical offering contrasted sharply with the tang of labouring bodies in a hot climate and a confined space. As we came out, and Clara put her shoes back on by the front door, Mimi, the school dinner lady, would be sitting reading about Johnny Halliday's comeback, or Carla Sarkozy's pregnancy wardrobe. There was one back copy of *Paris Match* with the singer who'd died of CF on the front. It was probably about five years old. Whenever I could I put it to the back of the rack, to reduce the chances of Clara seeing it next time we came in, but it seemed to work its way to the front every time.

On the way back to school at 2 p.m., everything was shuttered except the chemist's. The canvas awning was down over the fruit and vegetables outside the little supermarket. The owner of the shop that sold everything and nothing had pulled the racks of inflatable water toys and rubber shoes inside. The whole village seemed to shallow-breathe in rhythm during its long post-prandial snooze.

'How was it?' whichever of us hadn't accompanied Clara would ask the other. 'OK.' 'Not great.' 'Usual.' We seemed to have no other words for it than these. We should perhaps have just used fingers and thumbs or hand gestures, or written scores out of ten on a piece of paper on the fridge door.

After maybe three years of this routine the cystic fibrosis department in the university hospital held an all-day seminar for parents of children with CF, to update us on new physio techniques. I had scarcely ever knowingly met anyone from a family with cystic fibrosis. When we first started attending Tuesday clinics at Great Ormond Street all the children used to wait and play together in one big open waiting room, but shortly after we joined it was suggested that this was a dangerous practice, with a good chance your child would come home from their check-up with a potentially life-threatening bug they hadn't had when they walked in. After that all the appointments were scheduled separately and most of the contact between families took place either on fund-raising runs, when you hadn't much breath for small-talk, or on the online forum, which many of us found too difficult to handle.

It was extremely unusual for us to leave the children overnight. It was difficult for Clara to take all her pills and do her nebuliser and sterilise it and fit in a session of physio. At that time she was still fairly unselfconscious about the number of pills she took – other children would gather round to watch her throw nine pills down her throat at one go. A week before the CF seminar, when she'd been having dinner at the house of a friend, she put her pills beside her plate, having carefully counted them out. As usual there was an embarrassed silence, as Clara calmly reached for the water jug. '*Tu prends tout ça?*' the father said as they sat down to eat. '*Moi*, I don't take medicines. I don't believe in it. I'd rather trust my own body to do the work. There's too much dependence on antibiotics. *Ça va finir mal.*' 'Do they actually think I *like* taking them?' Clara exclaimed after repeating this to me, and my first thought was that an adult would have to be utterly crass to say such a thing to a child with a serious illness, and my second thought was that he would have to have a degree of malice too. Nico said no, people were just thoughtless. They wouldn't understand how it sounded to us.

While we went off to the seminar the children were staying with their godfather, David, who had come to live in the village, so we knew they would be at ease, as he was happy to let them back-comb his hair and tie it up in a quiff with a red ribbon and would read to them in a solemn voice from a Polish edition of *Some Freshwater Fish of the Southern Hemisphere* – he too was a translator – before leaving them to go to sleep to a harpsichord sonata by Couperin or some Russian techno music a former girlfriend had introduced him to. It was never dull.

We had so rarely left them that to be going away for a night, without the prospect of a hospital check-up the following day, or a flight and a visit to the home to see my mother, was like a trip you might win in a competition. Nico and I slept in a motel on a roundabout. You never seem to be far from a roundabout in France. We had croissants, like real holidaymakers, and walked round the shrubbery screening the motel from the juggernauts that tilted and straightened as they took the curve.

At the seminar we sat in a horseshoe and I looked round at the other parents, maybe thirty of us. Some couples. Two children, to my surprise, seated at the maximum possible distance apart: one the little English boy, Jack, and a girl in her mid-teens. She was a dancer and a swimmer, and looked astonishingly like Clara, so that on learning she had CF we were almost drawn into wondering whether we weren't related to her. We were, of course, related to all of these people. One in twenty-five people carries the recessive gene. One tiny portion of a minute sequence of DNA on the seventh chromosome of each of us contained a misprint; each of us qualified for a little erratum slip. We introduced ourselves, explaining why we were there. We were all there for the same reason, of course. One man said, 'My wife and I have split up, I only see my daughter once a month, I don't know how to do this for her. If I don't know how to look after her my wife will stop me seeing her.' A woman said, 'I live in the Pyrenees. My house is full of mould and rot and there's a pond in the garden. Should we move?' Her neighbour said, 'My daughter's fifteen, she won't admit she's got this illness, she won't do any physio at all, she stays in her room all day.' We were like any group of people with a passion who have suddenly found other people who share it – everything about it was interesting to us, a lot of it terrifying.

The man who was leading the seminar was from the nation-wide organisation of respiratory physiotherapists. Some of the physios from the children's hospital sat in and were obviously not very approving of him. He had a good patter, and asked snappy rhetorical questions that made us giggle and look down at our pieces of paper where we had written things like *best three hours after eating* and *trampolines – one in ten children severe breakages each season. Pelvic floor?* When he announced he was going to show a short film of the inner workings of a pair of afflicted lungs the young dancer got up and left the room, walking beautifully, with her back straight and a lightness in her step that owed something to the fact that, like Clara, she was by other girls' standards enviably underweight. I kept finding myself looking at her empty chair. I could see Jack starting to wriggle. He had the careless grace that is often the expression of impatience in older children. Our anxiety, our intentness on doing well, on learning, on being good late learners in our little chairs, looking studiously at the PowerPoint, scarcely fidgeting, hands clasped in front of us, phones off, must have seemed somehow puerile to him. His mother, Stephie, drew distractedly and, knowing she was a ceramic artist, I wondered if she was drawing pots, or alveoli and the endlessly ramifying labyrinth of a pair of lungs. I had drawn them myself in my last – purely theoretical – encounter with the concealed workings of the human body, in biology, little thinking I'd be sitting in France updating it – in French – many years from then.

When I was at school O-level French oral consisted of one hundred questions and answers which you wrote out and learned by heart. Question 1 (*La Maison*) was '*A quoi sert un aspirateur?*' ('What is a vaccum cleaner for?') – not a very thorough preparation for speaking everyday French. In Paris with my brother, just before I went to university to read French, I asked for *une chambre avec deux lits*. '*C'est votre petit ami?*' '*Non, monsieur, c'est mon frère.*' '*Ah, oui, c'est ça.*' As the man blushed for my naïvety at thinking him so naïve himself, I stuttered awkwardly, '*Eueh . . . combien . . . euh, quels sont les frais?*' – 'How much do you charge?' – at which he stopped laughing and looked at me a little more closely, wondering who exactly was having the last laugh.

By now my spoken French, through many years of practice in areas other than the discussion of existential despair, the effect of the moon on the surface of lakes, the *démesure* of

Horatio on the bridge, not to mention the vacuum cleaner, was good enough to deal with anything a be-toupéed respiratory physio might throw at me in a PowerPoint presentation. It was almost as advanced as my knowledge of the many varieties of pulmonary disease.

We broke for lunch. In the canteen Jack, by this time swooning with boredom and hunger, filled his tray with cold meat, *crudités*, chips, sausages and chocolate cake and sat down. We all began to eat, and I noticed after a minute or so that he had laid down his fork and was sitting looking worriedly at his food. Stephie looked over at him. 'OK?' He sighed heavily, and got up to fetch a glass of water. Came back. Took his enzymes. Tried a chip. Put half of it back down on his plate. Nico and I looked at each other. It was tiny things like that that overwhelmed us. Clara would have done exactly the same.

I cleared away my tray, scraped my bits, as one did at school. People began to gather by the door to walk back to the conference room, where, the teacher said, we would be practising on each other. I found myself anxiously seeking to meet Nico's eye, to check I could be his partner. What if no one wanted to pump my chest? *Loser!* Nico grinned at me and nodded over to where Mr Respiratory Physio was leading the group back to the other building. Women, since it was predominantly a mothers' gathering, walked either side of him, arms folded tight across their chests, in high heels mostly. Stephie and I were plain English, and the Frenchwomen were keeping the side up. Jack was hungry. We were tired. The edge of the city, the hospital grounds were all a building site, and it was hot and dusty. We were putting in our hours learning what we could. You never knew. As we reached the conference block the seminar leader held the door open for us. 'Laydeez!' he said, gallantly but with a slightly disparaging sweeping glance that took in our clothes and our slubby Cath Kidston bags full of tissues and phone chargers and notebooks. He let the door close behind us, remaining outside, and as I glanced back through the glass I saw him snatch a cigarette from a packet and duck to light it and draw as though his life depended on it. That single needful gesture seemed to be from a completely different repertoire, unrelated in any way to the body language out of a catalogue that he had displayed until now. We waited politely and when he returned no one mentioned it. It was strange to sit in a room that smelled of cigarette smoke. None of us, I guessed, would have done that since our children were born.

It wafted me back to previous parts of my life, and I wondered whether for many of the others it wasn't the same. When we used to take Clara to Great Ormond Street, we'd pick Nico up from his office in Senate House and walk across Russell Square Gardens. On the street in Kingsway and in Russell Square, people observing the recently introduced smoking ban for workplaces stood out on the pavement, inhaling and exhaling deeply, and Clara, so small then, but walking, would be just at the height of a cigarette held loosely in the hand while the smoker chatted. Eventually I took to letting her ride on my shoulders, elevating her to a cleaner air zone.

I don't think the practice that afternoon made any difference. We picked up a few tips and took them back to Eric, like anxious birds returning to the nest with worms in our beaks, but they were not followed up. I suppose we understood a bit better what they were trying to achieve, and when we returned to England and were again made responsible for Clara's daily physio, I remembered having my hand on Nico's chest that afternoon, and feeling it rise and fall as he breathed. He is the one who usually accompanies Clara in her daily breathing routines, his hand lightly on her back, just feeling her lungs rise and fall. He has healing hands, I have no doubt about that.

When I consider the different types of physiotherapy we have been taught for lung clearance, they seem to represent progress of sorts. The percussive action, we were told when we arrived in France, had long since been considered useless, except for the purpose of gaining a child's co-operation and teaching them to accept treatment. It was a gentle, rhythmic tapping, and babies and young children usually enjoy close physical contact. With Eric we entered a system – a generous, well-funded system – of physios and nurses, the absolute regime of French state provision, with, at times, too little breathing space for individuals. He applied pressure to her ribcage, squeezing and shaping her lungs, almost kneading them. The autogenic drainage system, based on breathing cycles, now quarter-filling her lungs, now half, now completely, was something new. The subject becomes autonomous, no longer a patient. The aim is that the body should use the natural process of breathing to the greatest possible effect, to feel what is happening in the lungs and follow those organs' best instincts. Nico's many years of yoga practice, with which he balanced his academic life, teaching it in a boys' prison, in a doctor's surgery and latterly a group in the village, had led him to this: to stay by his daughter while she breathed, his hands guiding her breath, in harmony with her.

Ma mignonne,
Je vous donne
Le bon jour;
Le séjour
C'est prison.
Guérison
Recouvrez,
Puis ouvrez
Votre porte
Et qu'on sorte
Vitement,
Car Clément
Le vous mande.
Va, friande
De ta bouche,
Qui se couche
En danger
Pour manger
Confitures;
Si tu dures
Trop malade,
Couleur fade
Tu prendras,
Et perdras
L'embonpoint.
Dieu te doint
Santé bonne,
Ma mignonne.

Clément Marot, 'Ma Mignonne'

Fair young friend,
I now send
my good-day;
shut away
you're a slave.
But be brave:
get well soon,
leave your room,
open doors,
do not pause,
if you've heard
Clement's word.
He says, 'Go,
sweet-toothed, so
raise your head
from your bed!
Don't deplete,
go and eat
sweet delights;
illness blights
your pink face
if it stays,
disturbing
your curving
silhouette.
May God let
sickness end,
fair young friend.

Clara's best friend was a small boy her own size. The two of them were a couple of sprites in a class of farmers' sons and daughters, and they loved and fought like a pair of celebrity newly-weds. They had imaginary games, which they played in the playground, threading their way through the footballs and under the skipping ropes and round the back of the girls in the top class who were practising talking about boys and pop music for when they would really need to, later on. They had a world with dragons and sorceresses in, parts played by the teachers without their knowledge. On the school cross-country race, though he was well ahead he dropped back, waiting for her to catch up, jogging on the spot as she coughed, leaning low with her hands on her knees.

One Wednesday afternoon when she was ten, Clara went up to play at his house, which had a commanding view of the village, and had been featured in magazines. When I got there they were playing on the Wii. I saw the boy making a mini-Clara, giving her features, a smile, some freckles, and she arrived on the screen, ready to play at the touch of the remote. It made me feel uneasy, because I didn't know then that that was what you did on a Wii. While I talked to his mother the children went outside, where it was beginning to grow dark and a strange blue light was already filling the valley, the colour of an early-evening cocktail. They lay out under the trees in the orchard watching the stars appear. Clara already knew she was about to go into hospital for the first time for intravenous antibiotics. 'I told him,' she said as we wheeled our bikes down the track. 'I trust him.' I wondered what she meant. That she entrusted him with this precious piece of personal information, as though she was giving him a present, or that she trusted him to keep it secret. She said, 'I was so happy, lying there under the stars.' Perhaps it is as with mothers and their children: you can be too happy. I told a psychoanalyst friend once that I had held Verity, as a very small child, in my arms, while listening to a song on the radio, and felt a kind of rapturous upliftedness, and she looked at me sternly and wagged her finger and said, 'Better not do it too often, though.' As though this kind of close connection would always be something you paid a price for. Only detach.

The following day Clara was checked into the hospital. She had her own room, to avoid cross-infection. There was an English woman on that floor, who sat with her room door open, and the nurses said I could go and talk to her if I liked. I went and sat on her bed and we chatted and I held her baby while the mother leaned back in a reclining chair and closed her eyes. I remembered the exhaustion that came from perfect vigilance over a sick baby, perfect attention to the minutest detail that might give a clue to what was wrong.

On the first day, Clara was in theatre for a bronchoscopy, during which the lungs are viewed by a camera sent down the trachea and suction is applied to clear any obstructions ('A quoi sert un aspirateur?'). On the second day we were given a pass to go out into the city. The spanking-new tram had stopped outside our room and we had watched the silver tube easing past, pausing, moving on, from the window. Clara had a line in her right arm that was connected to a flask like a baby's bottle, and she wore a sling – we were free to roam. We got on the tram. We'd forgotten her enzymes. We went back. We caught the tram again. We got out of the tram and went down into the underground. The train came in, we checked the destination. Métro lines in France have such complicated names, Châtillon-Montrouge – St Denis Basitique, La Courneuve 8 mai 1945 – Villejuif Louis Aragon. The train came in. Clara jumped on, I jumped on. We looked at each other. Her little face was grey from the antibiotics, but always full of life and questions. Right now the question was 'Are we on the right train?' We jumped off. Then I said, 'I think it was, actually, the right one,' and she jumped on again, and the doors closed before I could join her. The tube moved off implacably, and I saw her horrified little face scrunch up in a ball and people all around move in towards her.

Maybe every parent does something like that once in a lifetime, though probably only once. When we were in London some time later, Clara wouldn't let go of my hand or her sister's in the tube. We all had to jump on simultaneously, as though we were in some skipping game. Not because she thought she would get it wrong again, but because she was sure I would.

My first reaction was to tell myself to stay calm. It wouldn't help her to start shouting, and it wouldn't make the train come back. I knew there was some protocol, a procedure that people instructed their children to follow for such eventualities as this, but I wasn't sure I'd ever known what it was. As the tube slid off I had met her eyes and pointed down at the floor. 'I'll stay here,' I meant. 'You come back.' I think I gestured that because I couldn't improvise a gesture, in a split second, for 'You get off at the next stop and wait, I'll catch you up.' I stood on the platform and waited. Clara spoke

French, she could explain, someone would take charge of her. At the worst she could ask to be taken back to the hospital. No, no, that was wrong! A bad man would find her, or one of those hard-faced women you used to see in the identikit pictures in the newspapers. Her antibiotics would run out, she'd have no enzymes on her, they would not understand what she needed, she would become sick and they would throw her away somewhere and I would not know where to find her. Always, when these terrible possibilities crowd in on you, and the voice of reason says it is a million times more likely that someone kind will find her and take her to make an announcement over the loudspeaker system, there is the voice that says, Yes, but that's what parents always think, and it isn't always true. Just as when the voice of reason tells me no one will hijack the plane I am travelling in, shoot the pilot and fly us into a tower block, a voice says, Yes, but for some people who said, 'That's just not going to happen, not this morning, not ever,' it did.

These arguments were all flying round in my head, crashing up against the walls of my skull, as I ran over the bridge to the opposite platform to meet the first train coming in from the other direction. I stood and the minute hand of the clock moved once. It seemed to me that motherhood was one long vigil, was in vain. It arrived. People stepped off on to the platform, children with grown-ups. None of them was Clara. I stood, I was standing, I continued to stand, and the train left, and the platform was empty and my daughter was somewhere out there in a crowd, grey-faced, with a drip in her arm. She was somewhere in the world, out of sight, and I could not speak to her, or send her a message. She was out of my hands.

I ran up the steps. I could see from the way people stared at me as I flew past that I had the look of a woman to whom something had happened, and they shrank away from me. I dashed up to the *guichet*, where the clerk was looking through some papers. He held up his hand as I started to speak. '*Un instant, s'il vous plaît, madame.*' I said, 'No, I can't wait an instant, *je ne peux pas attendre, j'ai perdu ma fille.*' Even now as I write this, I can feel my heart pounding. My eyes must have been staring, my cheeks flushed red, the lines on my forehead deepened as though scored by a fistful of fingernails clawing across the skin. I looked at him, lowered my voice, tried to appear sane. '*J'ai perdu ma fille.*' It was such a terrible sentence to say. I gave him the details. 'We have heard of nothing,' he said. 'Go down into the station and wait. We will make an announcement.' 'She is only ten years old, she lives in the country, she has a tube coming out of her arm.' I must have started crying. '*Calmez-vous, madame,*' said the man. 'It happens.'

I didn't hear them make an announcement, but as I was about to go down to the platform again, someone shouted after me. 'They've found her. Go to the next station.' I ran to the opposite platform, up and along and down, and the train came in and I lunged on to it. The stops are very frequent, and in less than half a minute I was there. On the platform there was no one. I galloped up the escalator. In the ticket area there was no one. I plunged back down again, I must have missed them. No one, I went back up again. Someone watching me on CCTV must have thought I had lost my mind, not my daughter. I came back up to the ticket area. No one. Just as I was about to go down again a voice cut through all the other noises of the street outside, of the trains below, of the banging in my head, *'Maman!'* — a thin shriek of joy. She hurtled towards me, leaped over the barrier, with her arm and the bottle of medicine in the sling, and flung herself at me. The joy and exhilaration of being reunited was like the joy and exhilaration of birth, an agony of separation leading to the rapture of discovery. (I met a woman once who, in a far more terrifying situation, got caught with her daughter in the Boxing Day tsunami, and thought for a full minute her child had drowned. Then she swam round a rock and found her. She too said it was like giving birth to her again. 'Shall we swim back to the shore then?' she said quietly to her daughter, and they did.) In moments like these you feel a sense of momentary reprieve from all the awful possibilities life holds. Having brought my daughter through ten years of treatment, daily physiotherapy, nearly twenty pills a day, hospital visits and now intravenous drips, I was not going to let the bogeyman take her away. She looked up at me and I crushed my cheek against hers and held on to her with a fierceness that I recognised as the same fierceness with which my mother had held me after I'd fallen off a go-kart once, and cut my head open, and that I had mistaken for anger.

A woman came towards us a split second later. 'You see,' she said to Clara, 'I told you *maman* would come.' Clara said the lady had looked after her and taken her to the ticket office. 'I have daughters of my own,' said the woman. She looked down at Clara then stepped towards me and put her arms around me and I wept on her coat and thanked her while Clara held tight on to my hand. 'You would have done the same for me,' she said.

'Wait,' I said, as she turned to go. 'What's your name? So we can think about you.'

'Oh – Hélène,' she said, as though confirming what I had suspected all along.

When Clara came out of hospital she had to stay at home for ten days because the treatment was so exhausting. A nurse came twice a day and replenished the antibiotics. The first visit didn't go well. The nurse came in shouting, like someone in a play who has been told by the director, 'Now don't just get into character when you find yourself on stage. Start in the wings, it will be all the more convincing.'

'*Coucou, Clara!*' she shouted. 'Are you there? *Coucou!*'

Clara slid out into the hall and looked at her, with her back to the wall. 'Here.'

The woman introduced herself, and I took her upstairs to where a medical room had been prepared. She spent some time making up the medicines, drawing up saline solution through needles, injecting it into bottles of powdered drugs. Then she shouted, '*Coucou, Clara!* Are you com-ming?'

Clara rolled her eyes at me, and I shrugged. We both felt pretty despondent about the whole thing. 'Come on then,' I said. We went up, and she sat on her bed. There is something about medical procedures being carried out in your own home that makes them even more surreal. Never for a moment was I not grateful for the treatment she received; but it also made me feel sick to see the needle bin, a bright yellow plastic drum, waiting in the room opposite hers for the 'sharps', and to see the nurse don her green plastic one-use-only bib, and put on her plastic hat to cover her hair, in our house. It made me feel there was something toxic about my daughter, which others might be expected to fear. She was not healthy.

Therefore she couldn't be happy. I was a bad mother who had not sufficiently wished for her child to be healthy and happy. Though it could not be said that Clara was an unhappy child. When everything is OK she is radiant, with a particular kind of joy that is not like anyone else's. But when she felt ill, as she often did then, it was hard for her to be happy too. People like sick children to be meek and feeble, not grouchy and fidgety. But I was usually relieved when she began to get cross.

'We'll just pop this needle in — that's it, perfect, don't move, I'm pushing the fluid in now, I'm rinsing the vein, yes, it will be cold, be a brave girl now, it won't hurt, don't move or it will hurt, stop moving! It *can't* hurt — *ça ne peut* pas *faire mal*!'

'*Mais si, ça fait mal!*' She glared furiously at the nurse, then appealed to me. '*Maman!*'

'*Madame,*' the nurse said, 'this cannot hurt her. It is not possible.'

Then, 'Ah, the hospital have put the wrong attachment on the tube, so I have to force it like this . . . '

'Don't force it, it's OK. We'll go to the hospital and get the right attachment.'

'No, this is fine, I'll do what I've come to do. It doesn't hurt one little bit now, does it, Clara?'

'Yes,' she said in a minute voice. 'It hurts.'

'No!'

'Yes!' she yelled.

'Call the hospital,' I said to Nico. 'You,' I said to the nurse, 'just hold it there. Don't put any more of that stuff in her veins.' I thought she might cause some kind of blockage and something awful would happen. Nico got the specialist nurse on the phone. 'She says take her to the local clinic, give her gas, have it refitted properly.' So we got in the car and drove to the nearest town and they gave her delicious gas, which she loved; it was like heaven, she said. Then they put the tube in and attached the proper fitting and we drove home. The same nurse came back the next morning and Clara hid in the linen cupboard for quite a long time, which made more sense of the woman going round the house shouting, 'Clara? Where are you? Come on out now!' like the Child Catcher in *Chitty Chitty Bang Bang*.

Tout serait sans doute autrement tourné si nous n'avions pas consideré l'affaire d'une façon si mystérieuse et si tragique.

Everything would doubtless have turned out differently if we had not taken such a mysterious, tragic view of the affair.

Alain-Fournier, *Le Grand Meaulnes*

On her first day back at school, Clara was pale, her face very thin. She looked as though she had been out of the sun for years, not days. It was carnival day, and the theme that year was water. She was dressed in a cornflower-blue, silk-lined velvet cloak, with flowers in her hair. It was a little too Pre-Raphaelite, somewhere between the affronted innocence of *The Piano Lesson* and Ophelia in the pond.

'Why don't you just go as a sailor, like Verity?' I suggested, thinking, Don't stand out, don't be different, let it slide for once.

'What are you meant to be anyway?' Verity asked. 'You always wear that cloak, you wore it in hospital.'

'I'm not *meant to be* anything,' Clara said. 'I'm a water nymph.'

Each year the primary-school children trailed round the village, banging drums and blowing hooters. Constance had decided that year to teach them songs, and they stopped *en route*, a bit like doing the Stations of the Cross, to sing. The Monsieur Carnaval figure was dragged round at the front of the parade on a cart. He was made of newspaper and straw and dressed in the headmaster's old clothes. Each of the children in the primary school, around one hundred of them, had written his or her '*J'accuse*' note, which was pinned to his chest.

Monsieur Carnaval, je t'accuse d'avoir fait mourir le cerisier de mon grand-père! It's your fault my grandfather's cherry tree died.

Monsieur Carnaval, je t'accuse d'avoir fait la guerre en Syrie. It's your fault there's a war in Syria.

Monsieur Carnaval, je t'accuse d'avoir fait crever le pneu de mon vélo. It's your fault my bike tyre burst.

Monsieur Carnaval, je t'accuse d'avoir donné la mucoviscidose à ma soeur. It's your fault my sister has cystic fibrosis.

When they got to the river, a teacher with a petrol can and some matches set fire to Monsieur Carnaval and the children sang, *'Adeu paure Carnaval'* in Occitan as he was put on an improvised barge and pushed out on to the river:

> Farewell, farewell, farewell,
> Poor Carnival.
> You are leaving, I am staying.
> Farewell, poor Carnival.
> You are leaving, I am staying
> To eat garlic soup,
> To eat oil soup,
> To eat garlic soup.
> Farewell, farewell, farewell,
> Poor Carnival.

For a few seconds the river looked like the Ganges. As the little craft bore Monsieur Carnaval away under the bridge a black quiff of smoke lingered, so that it felt as though something was left with us that we had hoped to extinguish. The whole thing had the mournful feel of a real funeral, which it was meant to parody. I thought how much I hated carnival, its ticky-tacky greasepaint feel. I was meant to accompany the singing on an accordion, but it was so hot that the glue that held the squeezebox to the keyboard melted and all five kilos of it crashed to the ground, leaving me with just the cord around my neck.

The weather grew hotter, dryer. During the month of Clara's absence a change had occurred. The girls had begun to pair up with the boys. Now, each lunchtime while she was doing her physio there were snogging displays round the back of the prefab, boys with their hands up the girls' T-shirts, girls squirming on top of boys who lay on the floor, refusing to give back a stolen hairband or magazine. The teachers were only twenty metres away, but off duty. The little children came to look, peering round the corner and dashing away sniggering and blushing. Clara would come back from coughing up whatever was in her lungs, and take her place next to a boy who had just ejaculated into his shorts. It was the age of secretions. Some children began to pick up on the fact that Clara's lungs were filling up with sticky mucus, which would eventually stop her breathing altogether, and they spluttered behind her back and recoiled fastidiously from the thought of what physio might entail. Until recently one of them had sometimes come along to her physio sessions. So where did all that understanding go? As Clara withdrew into herself, and they grew into their very different bodies, the idea of her illness became frightening and repellent.

One day she found an old Dictaphone in my desk drawer. It had one of those tiny cassette tapes in, with an interview with a woman who had lived with J. D. Salinger when she was a teenager. I had recorded it while having breakfast with her in the Langham Hotel about fifteen years earlier. She'd finished publicising her book now, it was OK to record over. Clara loved playing with it. She had interviewed one of the nurses in hospital, getting her to tell jokes and talk about her holidays. She put the Dictaphone in her bag to take to school and showed a friend. The rumour went round fast that Clara was recording the other children secretly. She was a spy and was going to denounce them to the teacher! Already she had come home several times weeping and furious: 'They say I'm scraggy. They say you're stupid, Mama, they say Papa's old. Most adults,' she said, 'wouldn't believe how horrible children can be. Even the teachers. They've got no idea.' Her teacher said, 'She is not like the others,' and he made it sound like she was an unsatisfactory piece of work in progress. Her sister protected her in the playground. 'You're gonna DIE,' they said. No one else intervened, not even the little boy who had always been her friend, who had lain out under the stars with her and whose dearest wish not that long before had been that she let him spend the night with her in the laundry cupboard, dressed as a Dalmatian. 'They took my bag and shook it out, with all my pills, all over the floor. They found the Dictaphone, they took the tape out.'

'It won't be very interesting for them,' I said. 'There's just your interview with the nurse, and me talking to the lady for the magazine. In English.'

'They don't care about that. They say I'm a spy.'

'Ooh,' said her sister, 'I'd like to be a spy.'

Clara turned on her furiously: 'It's not a *game*.'

During that time, despite the hospital treatment, her health declined. The MRSA she had contracted in London when she was three flared up. She took antibiotics every day, but it never disappeared. Her liver was bloated, her kidneys were exhausted. I took her to see a doctor who lived on a farm up in the hills. She had been a regular GP, and was now more of a homoeopath. She had always kept an eye on Clara. Dominique got her to lie down, and then she just passed her hands very lightly over her, and noted what she felt. I had absolute confidence in her. I have had to quash whatever leanings I might have towards alternative approaches, in favour of the regular medicine that keeps Clara alive. But you would have to be perverse not to see at a glance that Dominique has powers other people either don't have, or don't know how to use. She used homoeopathy to keep Clara steady, to cleanse her system, gave her minerals and touched her in a way that made her body seem to breathe again: not just her lungs, but the whole of her.

'And you?' she said to me, when Clara had gone outside to sit with the dog. She told me to lie down and just moved her hands over me, as she had over Clara. 'You have a pain here?'

'Yes,' I said, and it was exactly there, a gnawing, rasping pain in my gut.

'So,' she said, 'you are worried. You think there is something wrong with you.'

'Yes,' I said.

'That you will die?'

'Probably.'

'And your child will be left, with no one to protect her.'

'Yes.'

'At your age,' she said, 'this is very common. You think you are the shield between your child and death, but it isn't true. You may even be shielding her from life.' We both looked around for some tissues, but this wasn't the NHS. Silversleeves! 'You must take this child away and find a place for her where people are kind and recognise her for herself. She is not going to thrive here. She is frightened and depressed.'

Where there is great love there are always miracles . . . One might almost say that an apparition is human vision corrected by divine love . . . The Miracles of the Church seem to me to rest not so much upon faces or voices or healing power coming suddenly near us from afar off, but upon our perceptions being made finer, so that for a moment our eyes can see and our ears can hear what is there about us always.

Willa Cather, *Death Comes for the Archbishop*

I became aware of an emptiness at the heart of the school. There was no artwork on the walls. I never saw a single story pinned up on the wall. If ever an exhibition went up, it was peculiar in that almost every single painting was identical. The interest might have lain in the minute differences between them, but the point was that the children had all learned, more or less, to do exactly the same thing. It is difficult to express what it is about a French school that wrings the neck of a child's creativity. The cliffs wrapped round the village, as one writer put it, like a wall of muscle around the heart, but in the school the arteries seemed to have hardened.

There was no talk of how we should try to love and help one another, only of how to be a good citizen. You learned about the structure of the electoral system before you learned about being a little ray of sunshine. Clara was not alone in being bullied – it happened all the time, but unless a school rule was actually broken or the principle of secularity threatened, no one was prepared to do anything about it. And even then the attitude was 'Well, it happens, they're children, that's the way children are,' so that one's rights as a person on the receiving end of bullying were waved away, and for once it suited the teachers or the headmaster and parents to say that it was the spirit of the thing and not the letter that mattered, and the spirit was you had to take things on the chin.

The bishop came to the village one December and visited every family who attended the church, and many who didn't.

He ate lunch and dinner in as many houses as he could in a week. He visited farms, watched ducks being fed, prayed over the old and sick and played with the children. Clara gave him a Silly band in the shape of a cross. Even Nico and I admired his intelligence and dignity, his willingness to speak on any matter, the quiet calm of his conviction; his goodness. Shortly after he returned to the Bishop's Palace an edict was issued sending the old priest, a stolid mother's boy whose vocation had come to him late in life, to a farther outpost of the *département*; to us the bishop sent Père Daniel.

He is young, and this is the first time he has had sole responsibility for a parish – for several, in fact: he is priest to seventeen churches and regularly gets stopped by the police for speeding. He teaches the children the car song: *Anges, chers anges, gardez-nous bien! Protégez-nous de tous ces fous qui roulent partout!*, 'Dear angels, protect us from all these crazy fools on the road' – meaning himself. People consider him a godsend.

I was introduced to him by Françoise, the Mayor's wife, when he was sanding his shutters on a table he'd set up in the church square outside the presbytery. He was wearing *bleus de travail*; you could just see his clerical collar. He always wore open sandals, no socks, even in the snow. His father had been a soldier, and he too had been at *école militaire* before going to the seminary. He was a vigorous young man, from a large Catholic family, strong in his faith, lusty for life and for God, intelligent and passionately in love with his calling. He had a parish, he had energy and a belief in the transforming power of love, the word and actions performed in faith.

The children dragged their heels on the way to the first catechism class of term. I never insisted they go – in fact it made me slightly uneasy – but I was happy for them to know their Bible stories and to have some sense of mystery. They came bounding home afterwards, wanting more. Père Daniel played the guitar and sang like a troubadour, he joked and clowned around, then suddenly a calm seriousness would descend. Transcendence went hand in hand with workmanship. Often Clara, in that climate, would say, '*J'ai soif.*' Père Daniel addressed the children's thirst, and it made some of the parents anxious. They wanted their children to be brought up in the Catholic faith, but Père Daniel's rapture exceeded the brief. After his first Sunday-morning Mass he stood on the steps of the church in his robes, a bit Scarlett O'Hara when she makes the curtains from Tara into a ballgown, but casting a certain radiance. His services were always beautiful: he was able to create an atmosphere of wonder and expectancy. The women envied him the fine fabric of his robes and the incredible pure whiteness of his surplices. Collecting the parents' telephone numbers and email addresses on his iPhone on the steps of the church after his first Mass, he turned to the wife of the plumber and asked: 'Where is your husband?' He was out beating the drum for the town band, elsewhere in the *département*. 'What does he do?' 'He's a plumber.' 'Name?' She gave it. He googled the plumber, then tilted the screen out of the sun so she could see it. 'That him?' It was. She looked at him as though he had performed a miracle; though he never managed to reel the plumber in.

At first the church was full every Sunday. Ten or more altar boys and girls gathered around the priest. He was much closer to them in age than he was to the mean age of his congregation, even with the new intake. But soon the figures fell, and a few months after his arrival people were saying that he had driven away more people than he had attracted to the church.

His message was simple: you do not love enough, you do not give enough, you are too attached to material possessions, your lives are not Christ-like enough. Your marriages are shoddy, you do not spend enough time with your children, you do not truly believe in God, and when you doubt you seek to modify what you are meant to believe in, not to grow in faith. It was easy to picture him at the heart of a charismatic revival, with his pleasant looks, his virility, his boyish humour and high spirits, his strong sense that things should be beautiful for God. He could be playful or stern, his standards were high, he tolerated no stupidity or hypocrisy.

On the first day back at school, just after he had arrived in the village, Sabine, the mother of one of the children's friends, met him on her way to the after-school drinks in the playground for teachers, town councillors and families, and invited him along. She introduced him to the headmaster. To give him his due, the headmaster shook the priest's hand and said, 'You will not see me very often in your church, but you are welcome in my school.' The next day, though, a number of parents complained. What was he? A paedophile? Why else would a priest set foot in a school?

The primary role of a school in France is to promote reason and fight prejudice. Secularism, not diversity and inclusion, is seen as the guarantor of peaceful coexistence between people of varied origins and faiths. It comes across as draconian and soulless. It can feel especially so to people accustomed to the view that society includes many people of no faith, and many people of different faiths, and we can all learn from each other, an unofficial mish-mash, governed by no obvious rationale. The separation of Church and state in France is one of those tenets that are proudly, inflexibly upheld. Many people affirm

it with all the ardour of a zealot. In public institutions –
schools, universities, government buildings – all religious
practices, discourses and symbols are outlawed. There are no
prayers, no religious songs. Christmas is about presents and
snow, Easter about bunnies. Nothing has yet come to take
the place of the deep humanity that for many people lies at
the heart of religion, just a kind of civic code of rights, which
nominally supports sexual and racial equality. Recently someone in government tacked on an awareness of bullying. It is a
dry, legalistic world, of '*J'ai le droit, tu as le droit, il/elle a/n'a pas
le droit.*' Some people think colonial guilt led to compromises
on the left, beginning in 1989 in Creil, when three female students arrived at school wearing the veil and were suspended.
The President at the time, Lionel Jospin, prevaricated. No one
has ever been quite sure since what is and isn't permissible;
each case is judged individually. Many people, though, trad-
itionalists, communists, feminists, the right, deplore signs of
slackening – in the case of Muslims, at least – on dress and
the display of religious symbols in schools, and accuse the left
of playing into the hands of the *Front National.* The arrival of
Père Daniel, flapping into the playground in his sandals and
cassock with his guitar on his back, was a provocation that
carried more meaning than was probably intended.

One summer the priest and his travelling theatre company
of (oh dear, lymphatic-looking) young Christians put on a
production of the life and death of St Thérèse of Lisieux, to
which he was keen we should take the children. Fortunately
Clara giggled so much at the sight of the consumptive Thérèse,
with the scenery collapsing on top of her at one point quite

early on in the show, that she had a coughing fit herself and had to go and sit outside to recover, soon wandering off with her sister in search of better entertainment. But what did the priest imagine might be the effect of such a performance on a young child who has recently learned that she is likely to die in young adulthood from lung disease? I was particularly irritated by the young Thérèse's persistent cough. Perhaps she would like me to get up and go and thump her lungs with the strange percussive movement we were taught to apply to Clara in London, long before the more enlightened, yoga-related autogenic drainage technique was introduced. I felt like giving someone a good pummelling. We did not wait for the scene of Thérèse's death, apotheosis, beatification or any of the rest. I was sickened by this morbid presentation of illness as a refinement, a consumption devoutly to be wished. There was Christ, suffering on the cross behind the spectacularly limp Thérèse as she hacked genteelly away; not a symbol of torture or suffering, remember: an image rather of joy and forgiveness.

After a few weeks, Père Daniel began to mention Clara's name in the prayers of intercession. After a few more weeks she asked him not to. The idea of the congregation, many of whom she felt had more problems than she did, praying for her, and some celestial board meeting deciding whether or not to grant a miracle, was too much. Some of the children praying for her on a Sunday were her persecutors in the play-ground on a Monday.

'If Clara can learn to forgive her persecutors perhaps she will get well,' Sabine said after Mass one Sunday, drawing on her gloves. She always brought a touch of Grace Kelly to the pews; on Mondays she was back in her dungarees, making pots.

'Does she really believe that nonsense?' I asked Nico. Clara wanted justice, she didn't want to become meek and holy, and I was pretty sure justice would do her a lot more good. Too much of that kind of anomaly and she would end up boycotting church altogether, which she did, even after Père Daniel stopped naming her in prayers and referred to her simply as 'a child of this parish'. At that the children gathered round the altar rail would nudge each other and the child next to Clara would dig her in the ribs, in case she hadn't realised they were bending the ears of the saints for her benefit. It made it worse, taking her name out, because people always thought, Which child? Why?; or, if they knew, wondered reasonably whether there weren't other children who were equally in need of prayer.

One day Clara said, 'Père Daniel says he is praying for a miracle for me.'

'We are all praying with him,' I said.

'What, that I'll get well?'

'No, that Frédéric Boussier will get trampled by a cow.'

She smiled only a little. 'He thinks Sainte Thérèse will cure me.'

'De Lisieux or Avila?' As we might have said, 'Bread from Léger or Piermont? Meat from Duval or Paulan?' It was important to spread your business between the *commerçants* of the village, not to patronise only one of the butchers or bakers.

'Lisieux, I think. The one who had tuberculosis.'

Oh dear, I thought. I should have seen that coming. I didn't want Clara to believe that a miracle could cure her. I said I felt that if a miracle occurred it would be due to the commitment and love of the people who cared for her and those who did medical research. I say 'love', because so many of the doctors and researchers who were looking for a cure, whether through gene therapy or some other treatment, seemed to be doing it because they desperatcly wanted to help the 70,000 people in the world whose daily lives were blighted by what all the publicity material calls 'this terrible disease'. The figures were imprinted in my mind now. Seventy thousand sufferers world-wide. Many do not survive into adulthood. Mean survival age: thirty-seven years. Cause of death: drowning in your own mucus. It's amazing anyone ever managed to raise any funds through charitable efforts really, it sounds so awful. And yet all over the world people were cycling, singing, abseiling, running marathons, almost always some kind of extreme physical effort, as though the strengthening of their bodies could indirectly connect with the bodies of the sufferers, and often the very doctors involved in treating the people afflicted with the disease were among the fund-raisers. I suppose they had more experience of its 'devastating effects' than most people. Clara said she thought the priest believed that if she was good enough and holy enough she would be cured.

I stopped off at the presbytery one morning and asked him if this was really what he thought. He laughed and said no, but that he prayed for her cvery day, several times, and that God listened and his prayer would be answered. As well as to God he also prayed, as a sort of 'cc', to Ste Therèse de Lisieux and the Blessed Agathe, who had been decapitated in the Revolution and had gone to the guillotine singing in a handcart.

It is difficult to write about, because prayer and hope and love all seem to occupy an area that has no mass, no shape, no weight, no outline. I do not know exactly what Père Daniel meant by a miracle. I was horrified by the thought that Clara might interpret his asking God to intervene to cure her as an admission that God had allowed her to have cystic fibrosis in the first place. The consideration of illness as a judgement on an individual, for their own faults or those of their ancestors, is surprisingly prevalent.

Quelqu'un était forcément responsable, rien ne se produit sans raison.

Someone must be responsible. Nothing happens for no reason.

Marie Darrieussecq, *Naissance des fantômes*

When Clara was diagnosed my cousin said, 'You didn't deserve this.' By this she meant, *You've done OK, you've looked after your parents, you've had a hard time on and off, why would this happen to you?* Both she and I knew that it was a casual remark intended to express sympathy, that's all. But the way I heard it, it carried other implications. That one's child might be born ill because one had sinned earlier on in one's life, done real harm to others. Tick. That one's way of life was in need of a corrective – I had been too free, too irresponsible, couldn't settle down with anyone, couldn't make a home. Tick. That one of one's ancestors needed to be taught a lesson in humility and difference, in being less than perfect. Tick, I think. Funnily enough, although many people report that when their child was diagnosed with CF they felt guilt, it had not occurred to me until then to feel guilty, either for transmitting the faulty gene to her, or for being attracted to another member of the adult population who carried a gene for CF, neither of which I felt I could have done anything about, particularly as pre-natal screening was not available then.

But as Clara's health began to deteriorate, I did begin to wonder about the question of deserving it. *'C'est bien fait pour toi!'* the French say, meaning 'It serves you right', and perhaps that it is closer to what I felt. It was 'well made for me'. It was particularly well made for me, I felt, since as a professional translator faithfulness, transmission and interpretation were my stock-in-trade. It was not well made, however, for Clara, who was the one to have to bear it. Some would say perhaps she had done something in a previous life that required this punitive corrective. It doesn't bear thinking about, the nasty idea that one's child might bring such baggage into the world. All these ideas are attempts to give meaning to the illness, where there is none.

I cherish certain moments in my life where people unexpectedly gave me insights that helped me to cope with the reality of things, to accept it. A Swiss woman living in France – she offered beds to pilgrims walking the Camino de Santiago – told me she'd had a baby daughter twenty years ago who had died of sudden infant death syndrome (cot death) on Christmas Eve, just before her first birthday. 'People said to me, "You must think all the time, Why me?" But I don't ever think that,' she said. 'I think, Why *not* me?' I had never heard anyone say this before. It made complete sense.

There is a meaning (it might also, perhaps more correctly, be described as an unexpectedly positive side-effect) to be hewn from the hard rock of helping a child to grow while it is carrying a burden greater than that of most people in the society in which it lives. In his book *Far from the Tree* Andrew Solomon says, 'One study found that most parents with disabled children surveyed believe that this has brought them closer to their spouse, their family members, and friends; taught them what's important in life; increased their empathy for others; engendered personal growth; and made them cherish their children more than if he or she had been born healthy.' Yet another survey found that 88 per cent of parents of children with disabilities felt happy when they thought about their child. Four out of five agreed that the disabled child had made their family closer, and a full 100 per cent endorsed the statement 'I have increased compassion for others due to my experience.' So does that mean that as we manage to control or eradicate most forms of physical disability or illness we will become progressively less compassionate? And that a plausible explanation for man's persistence in creating problems where none exist – climate change, war, violence, child abuse – is that somehow it is a spur to societies to engender altruism in a way that caring for the sick once did?

One of the odd things about Clara's illness was that most of the time you couldn't see she was any different from anyone else. Her looking like everyone else gave rise to a persistent rumour (which was balanced by the rumour that she was going to die when she was twenty-one, so you could take your pick) that she was not ill at all, just skipping school and trying to get sympathy. Apparently it is a good thing if the child looks 'normal': the parent is more likely to look after a child well if it looks like them. Even bullying parents are less likely to bully the one of their brood that closely resembles them.

There is something ethereal about a sickly child, of course. From the Romantics onwards it became fashionable to think of TB sufferers as super-sensitive beings (e.g. Emily Brontë, Poe, Chekhov, Kafka, Katherine Mansfield, D. H. Lawrence). Susan Sontag, in *Illness as Metaphor*, contrasts the glamorisation of the TB sufferer's pallor and thinness with the widespread repudiation of the cancer sufferer. 'A disease of the lung,' she says, bizarrely to my mind, 'is, metaphorically, a disease of the soul. Cancer, as a disease that can strike anywhere, is a disease of the body.' The TB sufferer might languish delicately at home writing poems, or become a kind of aristocratic drop-out, an exile travelling the world in search of the environment that might bring relief, a high, thin-aired,

Nietzschean environment. At the time these myths evolved it was not known (or, because of the persuasiveness of the myth, not acknowledged) that TB was actually bacterial. Was it entirely in the eye of the beholder that this sickness of the lungs, whose symptoms are in many ways similar to those of cystic fibrosis, lent the sufferer an ethereal air, appeared to spiritualise them, and in many cases to act as a spur to unusual degrees of individuality and creativity? For the Romantics, the hollow-eyed, skeletal look based on the tubercular model was a prime indicator of creativity and soulfulness, and Clara did draw a lot and write a lot of poetry, but I don't think she particularly cultivated an artistic persona, it was just that she felt safe drawing and writing, though neither happened at school. '*Ah non*,' she'd say, grinning wickedly as she mimicked the headmaster, '*on ne fait pas ça!*' While we lived in France I found that people applied to Clara many of the metaphors traditionally applied to TB sufferers. She was an angel; she had some higher knowledge; she was not of this world; she had much to teach us; she had been *sent* to teach us; she was gifted – and loved by the gods/God. Clara herself, given the choice, would have chosen gods, for their lack of sentimentality.

We never really wanted to explain or even describe the burden of Clara's treatments, because we didn't want anyone to feel sorry for her, or categorise her, label her as a sickly child. Perhaps as a result people didn't take her illness seriously. We kept it largely hidden. Occasionally I would allude to it, to explain her absences, usually, and I think people found that a bit unseemly – like a mother mentioning her child getting top marks in something, or drawing attention to its swimming prowess. In the end it comes down to knowledge, though. A couple of academics who came down from Paris to their house by the river every holiday had a son who was very suddenly taken ill and was found to have cancer of the stomach. We usually bumped into them at the market on a Saturday, but for a year or so saw nothing of them. When I did finally see Catherine, one Saturday afternoon in October, buying a pumpkin, I asked after her son. I understood he was slowly getting better. Her face was impassive. 'Yes,' she said stiffly, 'he's getting better.' I said, 'My child has *la mucoviscidose*.' It was as though I had muttered a code phrase. Immediately she looked up at me, gratefully it seemed, and her face relaxed. So I knew. We were in the same camp. I wasn't just *saying* I understood.

Human beings are so made that the ones who do the crushing feel nothing; it is the person crushed who feels what is happening. Unless one has placed oneself on the side of the oppressed, to feel with them, one cannot understand.

Simone Weil, *Lectures on Philosophy*

As the bullying got worse, we made a formal visit to the head-master. We knew him well. Nico and he had done carpentry around the village together to prepare for the summer festival, and we had an easy, friendly rapport. The teacher and the school psychologist sat in. What we didn't understand, they said, was that these were just children, being children. It was a rite of passage. An important stage in their development. She'd get over it. The school psychologist observed that Clara was an unusually kind, sociable and merry child. '*Ah non*,' the headmaster said, '*ah non*,' things had changed. She had only last week written a poem about a boy in her class, which was really most unsuitable. It was a four-line ditty which I had thought was funny and appropriate to the situation. I said I thought that children should be encouraged, within reason, to express their difficulties in poetry and painting – she had also drawn a series of 'Wanted' posters, showing the boys as gangsters, but had not put them up, possibly because she was aware that it might glamorise them and backfire. 'She is no longer the same child!' he said, confusingly.

'But,' I said helplessly, 'she is ill. She is—' Suddenly I found I was about to say, 'She is dying.' 'This is too much for her. It is crushing her, always to be alone, always being mocked.' The worst were the boys, and there were two of them, who had loved her. 'They told everyone about the dragon game we used to play,' she said. 'They said it was all my idea, and I believe in fairies, and I'm a baby. But they believe in what happens on

Nintendos. And in *adverts*!' She was, like many children who are wise beyond their years, both young and old before her time, in a sort of second, revised childhood. She had seen the future and it was not bright.

That evening on the way to choir Sabine said, 'And how did it go at the school, with your meeting?' I should have said, 'OK,' and that would have been that, but it wasn't OK. I said, 'Terrible. The headmaster is an idiot. He's always banging on about how he understands "the child", but he doesn't know the first thing about it. They think she should brace up. Hasn't she been brave enough already? When I see that child who's been tormenting her in his altar-boy robes on a Sunday morning, handing the priest the chalice, I want to throw something at him.'

'Those are the children who most need our prayers,' Sabine said smoothly.

'Really?' I said. 'Really? He's rich, he's well fed, he's mean, he's boastful, he's a bully, he picks on outsiders. Why does he need our prayers?' His life would be OK. He might get crushed by a cow giving birth to triplets, perhaps, and die tragically at twenty-five, but it didn't seem very likely.

'We all pray for Clara,' she said.

'Yes,' I said heavily, 'I know.'

'What do you mean? Surely you want people to pray for her? The priest says she asked him to stop.'

'It singles her out. The children all nudge each other.'

'They care about her! *You're* the one singling her out.'

'*What?*'

'Anyway, some children are just always going to attract that kind of attention.'

There were four of us in the car. One, the mother of

mixed-race children who had taken her daughter out of the local school after she was called a '*pute noire*', laughed and said, 'That's one way of putting it!'

'What I mean is,' Sabine persisted, 'that some children are just too sensitive.'

'Too sensitive for what?'

'She needs to learn. Not everything is lovely. Not everyone is kind. Life is hard.'

'I think she knows that by now.'

As we reached the turning for the village where the choir rehearsed, I said, 'There's nothing we can do. What's normal around here isn't normal for us.'

'Are you saying – it sounds to me like you're saying – we're not good enough? You think there's something wrong with us?'

'In England they call it bullying. It's a big issue. Everyone talks about it.'

'Then go back,' she said in exasperation. 'Nobody—'

'Why should we go back? Then what will change? Someone else will get bullied next year! Do you think it's just normal? Is "normal" good? You all accept the way things are round here, as though you can't change them. It's so – conservative!'

'"Round here"? "You" accept things? That's beginning to sound like racism to me,' she said, after which there was a long, angry silence. Antoine, driving the car, said nothing. His neck was stiff and solid, like a pillar in church. His child was one of the boys who had once been round at our house all the time and now had signed a piece of paper joining the We Hate Clara Club. We hadn't complained about it, but he knew we knew.

I said, 'How come you get all PC when it's about defending your own, and you sound like Maréchal Pétain when my daughter's life is at stake?'

'Don't exaggerate. This is absurd!'

'They take her pills out and throw them on the floor. They cough and splutter when she comes into class. Is that normal?'

She gave me a steady look and said nothing.

'You think I'm making it up.'

Nothing, still.

'You think it's all a story I've made up, because I'm angry she's ill.'

The mother of the mixed-race children was appalled too. 'You should consider it a mark of distinction,' she said as we walked towards the practice room, 'that they bully her. She is different. That's her strength. When she's a grown-up, if she makes it, she'll wear beautiful clothes she made herself, and that lovely reckless smile, and be an artist, and they will all want to say they knew her. But right now she doesn't fit. I know how much it hurts. And you can't afford for her to be unhappy. She needs her high spirits to keep well.'

I waited for Sabine. 'I'm sorry,' I said, 'I know I sound aggressive.'

'Oh it's nothing,' she said, and turned to talk to someone else.

We all walked over to the library, a shack on stilts that you reached up a flight of wooden stairs. The courtyard was busy with geraniums and the low ripple of excited male TV presenters purveying infinitely trivial thoughts to go with your evening meal. I got to the top of the steps, watched the others go through into the rehearsal room, turned round and went back down. It is a good thing to do, once in a while, to step back from a room you were going to enter without thinking. I went back down through the village and walked along by the river. Well, that's interesting, I thought. I've finished with all that. Whatever that spell was, that little fiction I was living out, the French village, the warm-hearted friends, the idyllic childhood for my daughters, that's all off now. The one thing that really bothered me was the thought that someone might get in their car and come and look for me. I would have hidden under a rock rather than be found and have them wheedle with me to go back.

How does bullying suddenly erupt? Is it almost always about the self-image of the bully, which he or she seeks to set in a favourable light by contrast with the image he or she creates of the victim? Is it shame of some sort that makes people run away from a victim? I know it sounds grandiose, but it does make you think of Peter and Judas, and perhaps that's OK, since they were just ordinary men. Were they ashamed to be associated with Jesus? Frightened for themselves, I suppose, that they would be contaminated by his unpopularity, put at risk by it? There is a wonderful book by the Austrian novelist Leo Perutz, written in 1957, which describes Leonardo da Vinci's search for a model for the face of Judas in his painting of the Last Supper. The idea is that, as Leonardo sees it, Judas betrayed Christ because Jesus did not live up to his expectations of him. Leonardo takes as his model a man who turns against a woman who rejects him, who will not let him satisfy his vision of himself as he would like to become. This is the look, he says, of one who has loved, and now denies it. Betrayal is not on any syllabus. It is certainly not discussed in citizenship classes. It is hard to know how we should learn it except, as most of us do, by finding that we have ourselves been guilty of it, and regretting it.

In discussions with the school and the parents of Clara's persecutors, there was a general feeling that she had to be seen to be unimpeachable before she could expect understanding. It reminded me of the bit in *When Hitler Stole Pink Rabbit* where the Jewish father, a professor who is about to flee Berlin for Switzerland because the Nazis have put a price on his head, tells his children that they must behave well in his absence. Jewish people, he says, have to behave better than other people. 'The Nazis say that Jewish people are dishonest. So it's not enough for us to be as honest as anyone else. We have to be more honest. We have to be more hard-working to prove that we're not lazy, more generous to prove that we're not mean and more polite to prove that we're not rude.' Reading that book to the children was helpful during the time when things were going wrong for us in the village. At one point Anna is being followed home from school and pelted with pebbles by some little boys in her class.

'Why did you chase her?' Mama was asking. 'Why did you all throw things at her? What had she done?'

The bandy-legged boy scowled and wouldn't say.

'I won't let you go!' said Mama. 'I won't let you go until you tell me why you did it!'

The bandy-legged boy looked hopelessly at Mama. Then he blushed and mumbled something.

'What?' said Mama.

Suddenly the bandy-legged boy grew desperate.

'Because we love her!' he shouted at the top of his voice. 'We did it because we love her!'

Later that evening I got an email from Sabine saying how much she loved Clara, that she was an angel, that every time she saw her she wanted to wrap her arms around her; she could understand why I was so protective, but that actually I was doing her more harm than any of her persecutors, who were just little children, testing their wings.

It is easy to say, but people did love her. They were touched by this slight child and her clear way of looking them in the eye, her determination not to be overcome by the illness that undermined her from within like an occupying, sometimes sedentary, sometimes restless force. Few people knew the extent of what she had to put up with. And I wondered whether the love that she inspired, not through being passive and docile but with her energy and curiosity and the way she engaged people and talked to them in all earnest, might not be part of the force that would work the miracle. There is, as I have said, the possibility that talk of miracles can work in a pernicious way. No one person deserves to be healed more than another, just as no one deserves more than the next person to be born with a disease. But I felt that Clara left no one indifferent, and many people said things like 'She's here for a reason' or 'She has things to do.' As she began gradually to withdraw from school life, though, to accept her hospital or home bed as a better place to be, we began to fear that these were not things she could accomplish in her present situation. None of us wanted to leave, but we wanted it to be different. And since that isn't really fair, and no one likes an outsider to stride in and start suggesting improvements, we had to consider moving ourselves. I had dreamed of a house, a life, a story, but I had chosen wrongly, letting myself be swayed perhaps by the idea of the thing, derived from other stories

and my own unfulfilled dreams. The realisation that I had
been wrong began to come to me after the *Stabat Mater* and
my mother's death. I was still writing our story. I realised that
it needed more than elaboration, embellishment, recasting. It
needed a new development, a rebirth.

La petite pomme s'ennuie
De n'être pas encore cueillie.
Les grosses pommes sont parties.
Petite pomme est sans amie.
Comme il fait froid dans cet automne,
Les jours sont courts, il va pleuvoir.
Comme on a peur au verger noir
Quand on est seule et qu'on est pomme.
Je n'en peux plus, viens me cueillir,
Tu viens me cueillir, Isabelle.
Ah! que c'est triste de vieillir
Quand on est pomme et qu'on est belle!
Prends-moi doucement dans ta main
Laisse-moi me ratatiner
Bien au chaud sur ta cheminée
Et tu me mangeras demain.

Géo Norge, 'Petite Pomme'

199

One little apple's rather sore
That no one's picked it heretofore.
The bigger ones have gone before.
The little one has no friends more.
The autumn chill cuts to the bone,
the days are short, the rains are near.
How the dark orchard fills with fear
For one small apple all alone.
I can't bear it, come pick me fast,
Please come and pick me, Isabelle.
Oh, how sad to breathe one's last
When one's an apple, fair and well!
Gather me gently in your palms
Let me grow old and shrivel soon
By the warm fire in your room
And then you'll eat me without qualms!

Towards the end of Clara's last term in primary school we went to see the headmistress of the secondary school. We explained that there had been problems with bullying, and asked whether perhaps Clara could be put with some new children, coming in from the outlying villages. Good idea, she agreed. Arrangements would be made. When the list went up, it turned out the class going up from the village primary was being kept intact except for four children, who were being put together in a different class: Clara and her three main persecutors. It was the kind of balls-up that made you feel the heart was cold, that there was no point trying to touch it.

On her last day of primary school, Clara walked in the back door, chucked her *cartable* in a corner and said, 'Thank goodness that's over, I never have to go back there again.' Verity loved her class and her friends, but even she could see why Clara was miserable. And Clara had stopped caring what anyone thought of her. She drew or read at playtimes, she accepted no invitations to play, she thought their gossip about sex and pop stars was stupid, since they had not much idea what sex was and the pop stars were just made-up people, really, and nothing to do with anybody, least of all the children round here, who didn't understand what they were singing and had never been outside the *département*. She saw through all the fakery and posturing of late childhood and by not joining in she challenged it in a way the other children found uncomfortable. She refused to backbite or bitch or wiggle her hips or wear a T-shirt whose slogan didn't have anything to do with her life.

Over that summer, whenever I suggested moving back to England, we talked about it a bit and decided it was absurd: we had thoroughly implanted ourselves here. Our home had become something rich and full of interest and life, the books and paintings, the children – younger ones, usually – dressing up and inhabiting its lost corners, the flow of friends through the kitchen, the singing and the painting: it was all part of something we had not studiously put together but which had grown very naturally and which we could not conceive of uprooting. We rarely went on holiday, because we had very little income, and when we went away we almost always came back early, because Clara felt unwell and needed home. The idea of moving her altogether was daunting.

We went to stay with my brother and his family, who'd rented a grand house in Provence where the swimming pool was cabbage-green. My brother said to the gardener, 'Can't you get it any better than this?' By the third day the children were desperate to swim, and the gardener had managed to get the pool to a less alarming colour; it looked a bit like clean washing-up water that you'd washed a milk pan in. Pools have to be absolutely immaculate, the water perfect, for it to be OK for people with CF to swim in them. The hospital said to avoid private pools if possible, but I saw the doctors thinking, Thank God we don't have to tell *our* children that, in these temperatures.

Clara was exhausted by the heat, and when her cousins fell into the water in relief, she followed. There were moments like that when I just thought, Here we go, it's just part of what happens. On the way home in the car, although Nico said it was too soon for her to show any symptoms even if she had picked up the pseudomonas bug we so dreaded, she was clearly less well than she had been on the way there. She always had a cough, was always productive in physio, but regular analysis of her sputum rarely showed up anything more than the MRSA. She looked so thin; she had almost no appetite, or sometimes a roaring appetite that vanished once the food was in front of her. She was still wearing jeans she'd had since she was eight, though they were short in the leg. She still wore the swimming costume she'd learned to swim in when she was five.

We heard of a school in a town not too far away. It was, like almost all private schools in France, a Catholic foundation. Private schools in France are not all that expensive. This one cost around 100 euros a term. It had very good academic results, being highly selective at the top end, but more interestingly for us, it promoted theatre, art and music. There was a cathedral choir which recruited from the school. Having always been rather smug about not having to be part of the great English conversation about schools, here we were, driving to look at a school sixty miles away, in a busy, hot and cramped-feeling town, because it had a choir and the staff claimed to understand the idea of pastoral care.

We walked down the main street. Verity trailed behind. Clara was excited by the possibility of a new place, new children; she had read reports of the school written up by other English families on the internet and was thrilled by the idea of meeting a few other Franco-British children, of not being the only one. Perhaps it would even be a school where the teachers were interested in each child being the best they could be, at the things they liked doing best; already Clara had been receiving *notes* for all her work for two years, marks out of 20, to be compared in detail with every other child. It was said that the teachers liked everyone to be as close to the average as possible. If you were below you repeated the year. If you were above you twiddled your thumbs. There was an emphasis on the class as a community, but not in any proper sense of the word. It just meant no special treatment for individuals, and in particular it seemed to mean the sacrifice of the individual to the common 'good', though that good seemed to be the Minister of Education's, that he might be seen to be doing his job.

The premises of the school were dreary, but next to a fine cathedral. The classrooms were tiny, the school less well equipped than the *collège* at home. But we had decided we really shouldn't send Clara to the local secondary. We would rent a small apartment and try it for a term. If it worked out, we would look into a more permanent solution. It was closer to the hospital Clara attended. There was a lovely primary school for Verity. Then we got back in the car and drove home. We had fixed something. Maybe it would work.

Nico and I returned to sign the children up for their new schools at the end of the summer holidays, leaving them to stay overnight with other families. Clara stayed with Antoine and his wife. Their daughter, Sara, was Clara's friend and she loved going there. But the atmosphere between our families had changed. There was no animosity, we'd just ceased to be active friends. I think it was partly because I had failed him in the concert; my heart hadn't been in it. And partly because Clara wouldn't go to school and we wouldn't force her. Perhaps they thought we set a bad example. The children's friendship persisted, though.

We signed up with the school, stayed a night in a pleasant enough hotel, but one in which the restaurant was far nicer than the rooms, which is never a good sign. We spent hours with a British estate agent whose daughter had gone through the school and was just off to university in England with a brilliant *bac*. We had an appointment to view an apartment in the centre of town, which was pretty and bustling and had theatres and cinemas and bookshops, and other children from beyond the *département*. It was a place where I could see the children growing up more easily. We were just on our way to lunch when my phone rang. I stood still in an exposed little square where no shade fell. All the walls were white, the heat made it difficult to breathe.

Clara was sobbing on the phone. 'I walked out, the boys kept trying to fight us, Sara came with me, we walked back to our house, we were just having lunch.' David, the children's godfather, had agreed to look after them all that day if they chose to come home, as I thought they might. Sleepovers are usually better in the anticipation, and the mornings after only good if you really, really like the person. (To be borne in mind.) Often we found it difficult to say no to Clara's requests, which were for innocent enough things but misguided by passion, in this case a passionate friendship, and being in love with the idea of friendship, and we let her steer herself into situations from which the lessons had to be painfully learned. 'Well, that's OK,' I said. 'Just make sure you have a good lunch. Is Sara there?'

'No!' she cried. 'Her father got home and found we weren't there and he came into the kitchen while we were having lunch and yanked her out and he was so angry, and now she's gone. He says she mustn't ever play with me again!' She was furious. I think it came from my father – she would not be trampled on, stood up for herself at every opportunity, challenged what she perceived as unfairness. It was exhausting.

'He'll get over it. I expect he was just annoyed because he didn't know where you were. He's responsible for you while we're away.' After I'd switched my phone right off I said to Nico, 'Let's just go home. None of this is going to work. What if it's us? What if we do all this and then it still goes wrong? We might as well just stay put.'

The next week, then, Clara, started at a third option: a secondary school in a nearby town. People didn't speak ill of it, as they did of the local school. We knew people whose children were there, in other years, and whilst it was beyond expectation – and would have been rather strange – to hear a French child say, 'I *love* my school,' no one actually complained of being abused there. It was a larger town, the buildings had some poetry, there was a good music school a short walk away. Going to the new school meant getting up at six in the morning, which was hard for her when often she'd been awake coughing in the night, so it was a good job it only lasted three days.

On the first day I went with her into the playground, where the first-years had been told to gather with their parents. There were about two hundred children, but we didn't know any of them, except perhaps one or two, just by sight. One child who had left the village school because she was being bullied the previous year came up and peered at Clara and said,

'I know you,' and turned away. Clara looked at me dolefully. 'I don't look like any of the other children here,' she said. She was wearing knee-length jeans and a striped top, but somehow it just wasn't OK. Then she looked at me and grinned. 'You don't look like any of the mothers either.' I hadn't worn heels or a cute little skirt or had my highlights done for the *rentrée*. Once I had tried to dress like a French woman for a concert, and my friend, who was always elegant and slight, like a comma or other small punctuation mark, an inflection, not a statement, said, '*Pas mal* – but no Frenchwoman would have her hair – so!' My hair was long and twisted in a knot that liked to think it said Barbara Hepworth, St Ives, 1949, but probably just said 'daughter's scrunchy, low self-esteem'.

Clara came back and covered her books that evening and said, 'OK,' when we asked her how it was. She came back the next day and said, 'Fine.' The phone rang the third day and a voice whispered, 'Mummy, come now. Please. Take me home.'

'What's up?' I asked when I got there. She was lying on a couch, curled up, in a sort of sick-room. A rather fierce and defensive-looking woman was sitting at a table, like a janitor.

'I feel sick,' she said.

'Have you had lunch?'

'No.'

'But it's two o clock!' People with CF need to eat as much as possible, as much of the time as possible. 'Did you have something at break?'

At break three girls from her class had positioned themselves on a wall opposite Clara, who was squatting in the shade under a tree, and watched her eating her crisps. Like I'm a horror movie, Clara said. Just eating. She should really eat crisps two or three times a day to keep her fat and salt levels up. Clara, thin as a twig, avoids their gaze, eats her crisps, her tiny delicate fingers and slender wrists back and forth between the bag and her mouth. She looks like a painting by Botticelli even when she's eating a bag of crisps. Eventually a girl slides off the wall and does her Beyoncé walk towards Clara, cushioned by the air pockets in her trainers, high on self-delight and the anticipation of a tiny little injection of satisfaction at a blow well delivered. She stops in front of Clara, stabs with her finger in the air. It is roasting hot, mid-morning, in a playground with no trees, where the stones have absorbed the Mediterranean heat all summer, where the light glances off the windows, and Clara can feel herself swaying with unhappiness, and dehydration. She wipes her mouth hastily as the girl leans towards her and says slowly, wonderingly, with exactly the right dose of incredulity and disgust: '*Mais tu GOUTES, toi!*' and slinks back to her friends. 'You SNACK!' They budge up, to make room for her on the wall.

'So why didn't you eat at lunch?'

Well, when she goes for lunch, feeling dizzy with hunger, she finds she doesn't have her enzymes, so she gives up her place in the lunch queue and goes to tell the dinner lady she needs to fetch them. We've written out and agreed with the headmaster a detailed plan for the management of Clara's CF needs. Promises have been made. Everyone is aware, it will be sensitively handled. The dinner lady says loudly, 'What? What pills? Where?'

'In my bag, in the cloakroom.'

The dinner lady looks down at the child. Why is she whispering? 'You don't have the right to take pills!' *Tu n'as pas le droit.*

Clara raises her voice. '*Mais si, j'ai le droit!*'

'Nobody told me!'

'It's in the protocol. My parents signed it!'

'Nobody told me. You stay here and eat your lunch!'

'I can't eat my lunch without them!'

'What's wrong with you? Why not? All right, sit down everybody. And silence!' To Clara: 'Why not?'

Clara shakes her head, looks down at the floor.

'Why not?'

Clara looks up. '*J'ai la mucoviscidose.*'

'The what?'

Clara mouths it again, but no sound comes out. She is sent to the sick-room, where she asks to be allowed to make a phone call.

The woman at the table is listening. We speak in English, but it is obvious what Clara is saying; besides, she has already told her this in French. I take Clara's head on my shoulder. I don't even know what to say, and I think the most supportive thing I can do is to show that I too am at a loss for words. The woman clears her throat to remind us she is still there. We just sit there bleakly. She says loudly, but in a voice that sounds as though I have just put a penny in the slot: '*Madame*, my door is always open. I am here to listen. I am the psychologist.' Clara mimics her afterwards, hilariously: '*Je suis LA pour ECOUTER!*' Wearily I pick up Clara's bag from the floor. Clara has great black marks under her eyes: Kate Moss *circa* 1992. I can see she is exhausted. She has had enough. When the morale goes, everything goes. 'But *madame*, my door is always open.'

'Yes,' I said, 'and I'm very glad to hear it, because we're leaving.' I didn't say, 'Stand aside!' but I could have done. In the car, even at the first roundabout, before we got out into the open countryside and on to the river road to home, I said, 'I will get you out of here.' I made her a promise.

For the next few weeks she didn't go to any school. She wasn't even enrolled in any school. No one reported her absence from any school she might have been at because they were worried there would be an inquiry by the education authority. Only Françoise, who taught her drawing, and the priest – who even though she had stopped going to Mass let her spend whole afternoons with him in the presbytery, answering letters from people researching their families through the church archives, and painting posters for the pilgrims, and sometimes just telling jokes or talking – took any notice of her. The priest had also visited her when she'd been in hospital; it was a four-hour round trip, which for a man with seventeen churches in his charge is a long time out of a day. She wouldn't go out into the village, where she might see other children. Not that many of them had ever been unkind to her, but she resented them all because even those who called themselves her friends, who expressed surprise and distress at her withdrawal, had not stood up for her when she needed it. She was not in a mood to forgive that reserve and was relieved not to be among them.

The long lower hall had not been lighted, and as she came downstairs, a last trustee stood, on the point of departure, in the open door that led to the porte-cochère. Jerusha caught only a fleeting impression of the man — and the impression consisted entirely of tallness. He was waving his arm toward an automobile waiting in the curved drive. As it sprang into motion and approached, head on for an instant, the glaring headlights threw his shadow sharply against the wall inside. The shadow pictured grotesquely elongated legs and arms that ran along the floor and up the wall of the corridor. It looked, for all the world, like a huge, wavering daddy-long-legs.

Jean Webster, *Daddy-Long-Legs*

A friend's nephew had recently started at a Quaker school in Somerset. A woman I met at a dinner up in the hills mentioned the same school to me. 'Go and see what you think,' she said. 'It may be what you're looking for.'

I took Clara to England the following week, to visit a number of schools within easy distance of a hospital with a specialist paediatric CF unit. We arrived at the Quaker school on the open morning, which happened to fall the day we were visiting. The main school was a harmonious white early-nineteenth-century building set in twenty acres of gardens, hills and meadows, with a number of Arts and Crafts houses on the estate, as well as the Quaker meeting house. The buildings and grounds felt uncannily familiar to me; I only realised recently that they match the burnt-down hall and estate buildings in the park in my childhood. (There was even a touch of the lunatic asylum of feeble-minded women where my father used to visit Auntie Edie.) There were beehives, vegetable plots, art rooms, drama studios, beautiful fields dipping and falling through woodlands where the sun touched grass that was soft and lush and yielding. A choir sang, teachers smiled and came and talked to us. Children were making pots and one girl had a horse. 'Please,' Clara said. 'Can I come here?' 'Not unless you have a benefactor!' I said.

I had visited partly to get an idea of what a school could be like. No, that's not quite true; I visited it because I believed that was where Clara would get well. I believed she was going to go there, even though we had no means of paying school fees. Perhaps I could write a book that would earn enough money to send both children there. I had never agreed with private schooling, particularly with the sense of superiority with which children seem to emerge from it. But I reasoned that no one would refuse the help of a private doctor on principle if they were in deep trouble.

We visited a few other schools in the area. I couldn't help thinking that the warmth, the interest, the unbossiness and the openness of the staff was somehow very British. We chose a state school near Bristol that seemed very good. The librarian said, 'You can come to the library any break or lunchtime and read.' Clara said, 'Really?'

The art teacher said, 'You can come and draw after school, if you'd like to. We have a club.'

'Really?'

The music teacher said, 'We have an orchestra and a choir. We put on musicals twice a year.'

It was amazing to us, that such things should be on offer.

After a week we had pretty much decided we would move back to England in a few months' time, and that the children would go to the state school we'd found. Most people don't have a choice, we had no choice; I had never had a choice as a child either, you just went to the local school and some of the teachers were OK and some of them were dreadful, likewise the children, and you survived. As we were going to bed Nico said to me, 'I don't see any point in going back to the Quaker school tomorrow morning. We can't even pay a term's fees in our present situation. It almost seems unfair to go and visit, to waste their time.' He was right. I looked in on the children last thing. Clara was still awake. 'It's late,' I said. 'We have to get up quite early tomorrow.'

'Shhh,' she said, 'I'm writing a story.'

I said to Nico, 'Let's just go anyway. Since we've got the appointment.' I wanted him to see what a school could be like. He had only known the inside of his own, hated, public school, and was still angry with it – he hadn't laid his anger down by the river, as he often told the children they should lay down their grouses and grievances, like the zen monks in the story, but was still carrying it around and bumping into people he'd been at school with whose burden and step were light as they sauntered across the green fields of England. Wolfing strawberries, Verity said.

The next day we returned to the school and met the headmaster. I was amazed, again, by the peace, the hushed drawing rooms, the flowers, the art on the walls. I could see Nico thinking it was like a boardroom and I wanted to say to him, 'I know you hate this atmosphere of privilege, I know drawing rooms and lilies make you think of Wagner and your own housemaster in the 1950s, but maybe this is different. Give them a chance.'

The head described the philosophy of the school, which is based on the Quaker values of truth, peace, simplicity, equality and sustainability.

> We cherish the truth which enables young people to develop integrity in what they do and what they think, helping them to build meaningful, lasting relationships . . . we believe all people are of equal worth and aim to build a truly international community that values all individuals and answers the good in everyone . . . we encourage our

young people to adopt peaceful methods of dealing with conflict in all its forms, taking both individual and collective responsibility in resolving differences . . . we believe in living simply and adventurously, placing charity and concern for others at the centre of what we do . . . we believe it is our responsibility to protect the Earth and to teach our young people to treasure it across the generations.

'I think your children would be very happy here,' said the headmaster after he'd talked to us for a while. I nodded, thinking it was a pity all schools couldn't be like this one, a scandal that they weren't. And wondering what we could possibly sell to afford even a term's fees. Someone I knew had recently discovered they owned a Lalique lampshade that had belonged to their parents, which would have covered a few years for both children. We had no lampshade, nor anything much to sell.

Clara caught my eye and lifted the book she'd been writing on the previous evening from her lap. 'Could Clara just show you something?' I said. 'Quickly?'

It was an illustrated book she had made during Wednesday afternoons with Françoise, telling the story of a courageous princess. It was the only story she ever told, really, unlike Verity, whose stories were more varied in their themes and outcomes. It was in French, but the colour in the illustrations was so vivid, they shone like figures in stained glass when the sun hits directly on the window in a southern church in the middle of a hot afternoon, and you could see, even without understanding the text, what was happening.

The child grows up in a country where everyone is her friend, particularly the animals. One day on the seashore, in a cave full of flowers, she finds a little boat. She runs to the chateau and packs her suitcase with scarves and dresses, adding in carrots for the rabbits and hazelnuts for the squirrels. 'All her friends wished to go with her. At last, they were all aboard. They didn't realise, but they were heading for a new world. The sea turned green. The birds began to make little croaking noises, almost like pigs. The birds tied scarves to the boat and pulled. And the boat rose into the air.' But though the sky is always blue, the clouds are violet, tinged with orange. A dragon awaits them in his lair. 'I am hungry!' he says. 'I want salt.' But Colette isn't afraid. She takes the most beautiful of all her scarves, lassoes the dragon and captures him, and at once he forgets his hunger and his anger. So now the dragon pulls the boat with the birds and girl and other animals all aboard, and they head off, to a new world.

I'd said 'quickly', but the moments during which he looked at Clara's story seemed like years we might have slept through. The colour of the illustrations was from the palette of the fifteenth-century masters, and I had occasionally thought Françoise must have access to some secret source. You could imagine a pedlar met by moonlight who offered hitherto unknown pigments against a first-born child, a deal done in the rapture of the moment. Later we were shown around the junior section of the school with Verity, who was cross and wanted to go home. A woman came to find us as we hovered by our car. 'The head would like to see you again, if you can.'

Nico and I were sitting side by side, he to the left of me, exactly as we had been in the consultant's room in the Royal Brompton when we were given Clara's diagnosis. The headmaster leaned forward and explained: a special fund of money existed that would pay for both children all the way through their schooling, so that our situation could be eased, so that Clara could be in an environment where she might thrive and be happy. The children wouldn't have to be separated, with one being given a privilege not available to the other. The money was made available in cases of particular need by one of the Quaker families who had made a vast fortune in chocolate. 'Like Willy Wonka,' Verity said later.

'I'll give you a moment to compose yourselves,' said the headmaster, as the doctor had years before. I looked across at Nico and saw that this time he was crying.

Père Daniel didn't seem surprised that the answer to his prayers for Clara should have come in the form of an open door to a dissenting, Nonconformist school where the only reference to religion came in the injunction to respect the divine in each individual.

On the way home I remembered that in *The Amazing Mr Blunden* there had been not only a park and a burnt-down house and a child whose courage had changed the wheel of time, but also a benefactor who had rewarded that courage and set the family on their feet again. Perhaps having your stories and believing them too really can change everything. I think the thing I felt most amazed and gratified by was the revelation that the clouds could suddenly swirl into a new configuration, sunlight could burst through, new hope, just as the reverse could happen, and happens to people every day, all the time. That both were possible. That you should always be ready.

Why, if one wants to compare life to anything, one must liken it to being blown through the Tube at fifty miles an hour — landing at the other end without a single hairpin in one's hair! Shot out at the feet of God entirely naked! Tumbling head over heels in the asphodel meadows like brown paper parcels pitched down a chute in the post office! With one's hair flying back like the tail of a race-horse. Yes, that seems to express the rapidity of life, the perpetual waste and repair; all so casual, all so haphazard . . .

Virginia Woolf, 'The Mark on the Wall'

Betrayal means breaking ranks and going off into the unknown.

Milan Kundera, *The Unbearable Lightness of Being*

Confirmation would take three weeks, but we should think about packing, because the school wanted them to start straight after half-term.

'We're moving to England in ten days' time,' I told Verity. 'Papa's found a little house on a hillside near the school. We can live there while we find somewhere permanent to move to.'

Verity nodded and said gloomily, 'I knew something bad was going to happen.'

'When?'

'In June, when she cried at the hospital.'

Clara's wonderful doctor in Toulouse had told us out of the blue that he was leaving. He was moving to Africa. 'So you won't be my doctor any more?'

'No,' he'd said. 'But you'll be OK.'

Verity was happy in France; she had her friends, she loved school, the village, she loved every day, in that way you do when you are in your place, even when things go wrong, and she could feel that it was all about to slide. 'You'll have a uniform,' we said. 'You can play hockey!' Clara said. And Verity, who never shouted, who always made way, who had learned from the very start to support her sister, and distract her, and sometimes even to lash out on her behalf, yelled, 'I don't want to play hockey! I want to stay here!'

~

The next day the hospital rang and said they'd detected pseudomonas on Clara's last sputum test. It was either the green swimming pool or the bat droppings, I thought. When she got an extra infection we always wondered where the crack in our armour had been. We had to observe what would previously have seemed to us unthinkably high levels of hygiene around the house, despite the dog. The children were almost unique, I think, in washing their hands before every meal. But you couldn't protect against everything. I felt like the knight in the hymn, 'a shield on his arm and a lance in his hand': bleach and kitchen paper. My hands were raw with cleaning. I was standing with my back to the wall opposite the portrait of the ancestress and the site of the *mise-en-abîme*, sliding down to the floor with the phone still in my hand. The dog came up from downstairs and sat next to me on the floor and laid her head on my knee. 'She needs to come in straight away for IVs.' That evening Clara and Verity ran me a lavender-scented bath, lit candles and put Bach's *Musical Offering* on the iPod. I said to Verity, 'I'm sorry, I don't really know why I'm so upset, I should be comforting you,' and she looked at me long and hard and said, 'Mummy, you've got to leave your home, all your friends, your job, and you've got a child with CF who's got to go into hospital in two days' time. You're allowed to be upset.' At eight, she sometimes seemed already to have learned everything she needed to know: compassion, directness, realism.

Clara answered the phone while I was packing for the hospital. I could see her face cloud, and she actually moved the phone away from her as though it was emitting a painful signal. It was Antoine's wife, just ringing to fix a lift for the girls to a music lesson. 'Ah, the *petite fille* who won't go to school. How are you?'

'OK, thanks.'

'And how am I?'

'What?'

'Oh, I'm very well thank you, *thank you* for asking.'

'What?' She handed me the phone, frowning. It didn't take much to upset her; but nor was she ridiculously oversensitive. People met their match in her because they could indulge in some small meanness and she instantly felt it. Everything registered. I continued making the arrangement, when Nico, who is not oversensitive and is passionately fair, came in and said, while I was talking, 'Just tell her we'll make our own arrangements.' So I said, 'Clara's upset. I don't know why. Was it something you said?'

'*Mais enfin*,' she exclaimed, 'what is wrong with the child?'

'Maybe,' I said, thinking I might as well, 'she's heard that you won't let your daughter play with her any more now she won't go to school.'

There was an embarrassed silence before she said, 'Well, that's just too bad.'

I waited to see what she'd say next. 'It's not me,' she said. 'Her father just felt it would be . . . better.'

'Well maybe,' I said, 'her father could just butt out of it for a while. She won't go to school because she's afraid to go to school, it's making her ill.'

'I heard she didn't like school.'

'She doesn't. But that's not why she's not going. Does it bother you?'

'Well,' she said. 'Well, yes it does. My husband feels it's wrong. Picking and choosing like that.'

'Do you think,' I said, 'that she chose to have this illness? Do you think she put her hand up when they dished out the genes? Do you think if your husband gets sick and can't go to work we should ban him from our house because he's setting a bad example? Are you crazy?'

'Oh dear,' she said nervously, 'oh dear. Oh, he's coming over now, he's heard you, oh dear, I'm passing you over to him.'

'Good,' I said. 'You do that.'

'So,' he said, heaving himself on to the phone. 'You're a writer. Write this down. Put it in one of your stories. I forbid them ever to meet or to play together. I don't want your child in my house ever again.'

Perhaps I am not overly given to forgiving people. If someone comes to me and says, 'I am sorry, I was wrong, I hurt you, how can I make it better?' then of course that's a different thing. But just forgiving people who don't even accept they've hurt you? I know it is generally thought that one should, but I can't quite see the point of it, except that it's meant to make you feel better. I can imagine getting over it, putting it behind me and being prepared to speak to them civilly or grab them by the collar if they're about to step out in front of a bus. But there's something that remains, a degree of wariness – maybe that's all it is, just being aware of what might come from that direction another time. Jesus said, 'Forgive them, for they know not what they do.' It is certainly true that most of the children who bullied Clara came into the category of 'not knowing what they did'. The difficult thing is forgiving the parents. And most of all those adults who know perfectly well what they're doing and do it anyway, repeatedly. Now, though, I realise that each slight remark or trivial act that I found so devastating, that made it so impossible to stay, gained its significance through accumulation. A throwaway comment, an ill-judged dismissal or failure to react, things that were not necessarily ill-intentioned or even conscious, all these aligned to form a pattern which I made into a plot – not in the sense of a conspiracy, but of a story with motivation and consequences. I constructed a story with a meaning, and that meaning was that we had to leave. It was a subjective interpretation on my part; which is not to say it was wrong. That is where the 'not knowing' comes in. No one else can be expected to know where your fault line lies. And that works both ways. All around me were people with fault lines, break-ing points of their own.

In hospital Clara was given antibiotics down a line twenty-four hours a day and did extended physio sessions to try to clear her lungs. She was very underweight and weak, but strong too, knowing that things were about to change. A couple of children in the village threw stones at her when she got home – or, more precisely, at the sling on her arm where the drip admitted the antibiotics from a bottle in a pouch into the line which went into her arm. 'You're an extra-terrestrial!' they shouted. Verity threw stones back at them, scrambling up on to the garden wall for extra height. I was pleased to see she was a good shot.

It had been planned for months that on Nico's birthday that year, his seventieth, we would climb Mont Ventoux. Petrarch, the subject of Nico's research and writing for several decades, climbed it in 1336 with his brother, and Nico had written a bit about his account of this ascent, but had never actually climbed it himself. Petrarch presents his ascent of Mont Ventoux as a defining moment in his life. We had arranged to meet up with friends from different parts of Nico's life, and all climb together. It would be the last thing we did before leaving our life in France and returning to England. But we had to cancel, because Clara was still on the drip and the nurses were coming in. Nico instead wrote a long essay called 'On Not Climbing Mont Ventoux'. Our friends met and climbed it anyway, but had to turn back because it was snowing.

That same day, Nico drove to a remote village in the Aveyron to collect a roof rack he'd bought on eBay. We hadn't sold our house, so all we were taking was a collection of clothes and books and, of course, medicines, but we needed a roof rack. Nico only told me once he was back safely that he had not really expected to make it. Petrarch had died on the eve of his seventieth birthday.

We gave a small party. The children sang a song to the tune of 'Can't You See' ('Gonna climb a mountain . . . '):

> Gonna climb Mont Ventoux,
> Not a little hill,
> Gonna climb Mont Ventoux,
> At least I hope we will.
> Gonna climb Mont Ventoux
> With all our friends.
> Gonna climb up to the summit,
> Then we'll come back down again.

Yes it's your birthday,
Three score years and ten.
I guess by now
You'll be wondering when
The peace and quiet
You thought would come
Will come over that horizon.
Well, just keep on dreaming, chum.

Papa, you're our hero,
Nothing you can't do.
You can write in Latin,
Mend a puncture too.
Oh gentle neighbour, please do not fret,
'Cause we haven't gone to heaven,
We've only gone to Somerset!

The last two lines were taken verbatim from a plaque on a
bench on Hampstead Heath which we used to pass when we
walked up to Kenwood with the children when they were
very small. The party was like a wake. People were shocked
that we could just decide to leave. Constance said to me, 'I
know you have your reasons but it feels to us like you think
we're not good enough.' I thought I was simply doing what
people have done for millennia, leaving to find a better life for
my family. In a way I felt happy, because I had not yet gauged
how painful the wrench would be, I was focused only on
making things better. Clara was out of hospital. In two days
she would be off the drip; she might even be well as a result of
the treatment, though that was never guaranteed. We would
leave for England; the children were due to start at their new

school the following Monday. The uniform shop was opening specially for them on the Friday.

When almost everyone had left we drank champagne with our dearest friends, who remained and toasted Nico. He had lived a day longer, at least, than Francesco Petrarca.

PART THREE

Moving On

Many things are beyond the reach of reason, and to seek to understand life solely through the application of reason is like trying to grasp a flame with tweezers. You are left with a piece of charred wood that immediately stops blazing.

André Gide, *The Counterfeiters*

A portrait of Nico's mother, Liza, painted by Nadia Boulanger hangs over the fireplace, with exactly the same tilt of the head that Nico has, the same half-smile. And in his study is a black and white photograph of her half lying on a *chaise longue*, with her hair done up in exactly the same way as it was in the portrait, which hangs behind her on the wall.

When he was seventeen or so, Liza moved from genteel poverty in Kensington to a stone house not far from the troubadour town of Les Baux. Nico, a lean, unhappy English schoolboy bound for Cambridge, took the train from Victoria, via Paris, in his holidays in the late 1950s, and learned to build walls in local stone, to do simple wiring, to dowse for water. What he really wanted was to be an apprentice to a potter in Les Baux; he went instead to Cambridge and three years later began a forty-year career teaching *Tristan and Isolde*, the troubadour poets, François Villon, Clément Marot, and studying Petrarch. His mother said that often, returning home after an absence, she would see a Roman soldier sitting on a rock set high and back from the road between Mouriès and Les Baux. And Nico's life has been spent, intellectually, between the classical world and the troubadour world, on that stony road where poems were often sung and seldom recorded. If he dies before I do, I will go and look for him on that road, and if I don't find him there I will go and look on the road between Siena and a tiny Tuscan village called Pievasciata; and if he isn't there either, I'll go back and wait beside the river, at the far end of the village gardens in France.

His mother – when I briefly met her in the quad of Somerville College in the 1980s, and then a few weeks before her death, holding our newly born daughter, both of them looking like pictures of the same walnut drawn with slightly different pencils – did not come across as someone closely acquainted with poverty. (Looking round her house for a gift for the baby, she found a glass butterfly; Clara has kept it, and regards it as a treasure.) But during her adult life she moved from Belgravia, when her husband left her for the woman next door, to South Kensington, where she was preyed upon by Jesuits and artists, and then to Provence, where she lived in the stone house with, for a time, not much roof. Her lover, I suppose you would call him that, lived in the other half of the house. Nico said he was a caustic, brilliant man, a writer and environmentalist. One day he hanged himself, leaving her nothing, not even his half of the house, just a note saying she was to blame for his death. Sometimes you glimpse a kind of unhappiness, or despair, that could make the bottle of pills, the floating away on a surge of current or even the leap into the void seem a better option. But then it is the drifting away into whatever comes after that appeals, the no longer being responsible, no longer the body or the psyche that carries this pain. Nico felt this man had killed himself because it was the greatest act of violence he could inflict on the people around him, lovers or casual friends or even readers, anyone who had failed to hear him call.

Liza came back to England in her sixties but lived well into her eighties, and is someone people remember with affection and a little awe. I recall a bright yellow scarf and smart pepper-grey hair cut in a French style, and a hawk-nose. Shortly before her death a Jesuit priest told her that he did not think there was actually such a thing as hell. She had lived all her life with that falsehood, and to cut free of it so late must have been both exquisite relief and desolating, to think one had allowed oneself to live a life distorted by artificial conditions, like an animal in an experimental laboratory at last released to spend its last few years in the wild. I think she grew to enjoy living in Oxford, but she never lost the feeling that France was the place where she had thrived and grown naturally towards the sun, and that everything else was a compromise. It is odd, really, because I think it is true for so many British people, this feeling about France, and yet France is not that country. People have described the Hellenistic spirit as an itinerant thing, now in ancient Greece, now in fifteenth-century Italy, then in eighteenth-century Germany, wherever it laid its hat. Similarly, France is not always the place where France is, which is partly why so many British people leave it. Our view of it is so partial, conditioned by representations of it that are not familiar or relevant to a lot of French people.

But I think that is true of most of life. We are often looking for things that do not really exist. Many times when I lived in France I longed for certain things English, the people above all, and certain kinds of landscape which can still be found here in Somerset at least, with winter trees and fantastically woolly sheep trotting dizzily across a hillside and a church tower reaching up between a fold in the hills. But really what I was looking for was the way such things make me feel, or had made me feel when I first encountered them in books.

In between Les Baux and Cambridge Nico spent a season in Italy. His Aunt June and her Italian husband had a family hotel on the shore of Lake Como, the Hotel du Lac. He worked on the reception desk, speaking many languages like a Central European, and had a sweetheart called Adelaida who had grown up in the town. When we go to visit Aunt June and sit out under the arcades after dinner, Adelaida passes, walking by the lake with her husband. She takes Nico's hands in hers and squeezes them and says, '*Nico, carissimo.*' She is still beautiful; she looks like Margot Fonteyn, with her hair pulled back into a tight black chignon, and wide swirling skirts and little heeled shoes. I think of them as a couple sometimes, a faint couple, ethereal even, but connected still. Nico's unlived lives and my own are multiple; our life now a fragile braid woven from single threads plucked from a skein of infinite possibilities. The threads that were never taken up seem to accompany us and give our lives substance and depth.

Around the middle of his life, Nico bought a small stone house in the Sienese hills, surrounded by olive trees. He spent almost all his time out of term mending and fixing the house, sometimes writing about Petrarch, sometimes sculpting, sometimes making a bomb of twigs and rags and petrol and dropping it down the chimney to meet another identical one coming up, which he'd lit in the grate. The confluence of the two sent a great whoosh of air shooting up the chimney, and the hornets' nest with it, sailing up Mary Poppins-like above the roof into the sky above the hills. Perhaps in Siena, drinking their *limoncello* on the Piazza del Campo, they saw him signalling.

He had earned ownership of such a house. He had lived with Petrarch since boyhood. Petrarch himself, though Italian, and born in Florence, had lived mostly in Avignon, where his parents moved with the papal court, returning only at the end of his life to the north of Italy. Some of our most intense relationships in life can be with people who are no longer alive. Sometimes, in the case of fictional characters, with people who never lived at all.

Nico's relationship with Petrarch has aged as he has aged. The other day, in the Italian coffee shop in Bristol, sitting on a high stool facing the wall, with Verity alongside in her English school uniform, legs dangling, drinking hot chocolate, he picked up an old edition of *The Penguin Book of Italian Verse* from a pile of books left out by the owner of the café as decor. He found the sonnet he had recited at school on Founders Day, and taught Verity to translate the first few lines: '*Solo et pensoso i più deserti campi/Vo mesurando a passi tardi e lenti.*' The Italian girl behind the counter mouthed along silently as she wiped down the zinc, remembering perhaps a favourite teacher who had intoned the same poem on a long afternoon in the *liceo*. It's a melancholy sonnet, in which the poet, tired of being 'known' only on the outside, retreats to a solitary, wild place, where he can walk alone – 'Yet no path is so harsh, so wild, that love cannot find a way to join me, and to speak to me, and I to answer.' There is a definite pre-Romantic sensibility to the poem. Petrarch's sonnets were written in the fourteenth century, in Italian vernacular, though his prose works were all written in Latin.

In Provence Petrarch is an ever-present figure. At a cathedral service in Avignon on Good Friday 1327 he first glimpsed Laura, who became the object of his love and desire and the inspiration for the sonnets for which he is widely known today. Nico has contended, in print, that Petrarch's idealising love for Laura was an artful invention, that over the fifty years he spent composing and rewriting the sonnets he probably never had much to do with Laura as a real person, and that she may never actually have existed (though she is often thought to have been the wife of an ancestor of the Marquis de Sade). And yet over the centuries Laura has inspired such devotion, and so many imagined portraits, that in saying she may not have existed and certainly was of no actual particular interest to Petrarch during his life is an act of literary rainbow-unweaving that Richard Dawkins himself would be pleased with. When Nico casts doubt on the reality of certain claims, or tries to discourage the children from building castles in the air, they turn on him and accuse him of 'doing a Laura'.

We had planned to move to Italy, not France, when Nico retired. But his wasn't a house where you could easily bring up a child with cystic fibrosis, and Nico put it up for sale. He is not someone who dwells on loss, he has a historian's long view; though later that year, when the removal van, with all his library of Petrarch books, pulled off up the drive, and he walked behind it as though following a hearse, he developed a headache that inflamed the inside of his skull and lasted three days and nights.

When Clara was first diagnosed the doctors insisted we should carry on as normal. It wouldn't help her, they said, to be overprotective. They had heard of families who wouldn't stay in hotels, wouldn't take public transport, or go to parks or beaches or playgrounds or shopping centres, for fear their CF child would pick up a bug. Take a bottle of anti-bacterial gel wherever you go, and get on with life.

So, since the estate agent was already pacing the floor,

calculating the square metrage of the house and counting the olive trees, we took Clara, who was by now nine months old, to Provence, with the bottle of anti-bacterial gel. We visited Fontaine-de-Vaucluse and looked down into the glassy green waters and I worried that the algae in the pool beside the Petrarch Museum would give her pseudomonas. She was coughing and pale, but her huge grey-blue eyes rarely closed and we rarely, any of us, slept. There was no question of our living in Provence, it was far too expensive now. We would find some other place, where the melons were smaller and the sun a little less fierce besides. Nico said he would rather not revisit his mother's old house. He didn't want to overlay his memory of it with new things. He had good memories of it. I did too, though I'd never actually been there.

One lunchtime we were sitting in the restaurant of the Café des Artistes in Saint-Rémy. It was one of those lunchtimes when you feel so ill with the tiredness that comes from looking after a baby, you just want to put your head under a pillow. It wasn't Clara who was unfit to travel, it was me. But I was glad to be sitting here, in a place that had associations for both of us. I had worked in Saint-Rémy only eighteen months previously, as a guide to Americans on walking tours, and had my base in a tiny room at the top of the Café des Artistes. We ordered our food and the waitress came and laid out the knives and forks and put a bread basket down on the table. Clara was on my knee. I gave her a bread roll to play with. 'I'm so tired,' I said, peeling the top off a pot of yoghurt, opening the capsule of pancreatic enzymes and shaking it out over the food. I passed Clara and the food over to Nico, and slumped in my chair. Less than two years ago I'd been sitting there at the bar, a single woman, free and a little lonely, not expecting all this – all this *love* to blow into my life. Shall we just go home to London? I wondered. Be safe? Shelter her from harm? I picked up my knife. As I did so, there was a loud bang, like the noise of a small explosion, a jolt zipped up my arm and the knife snapped in the middle of the blade, which was of a single piece of metal with the handle. I was left with half of the blade in one hand and the handle with the rest of the blade still attached in the other. Clara looked at me, I looked at Nico. He pointed over my shoulder and I turned around. On the window ledge behind us sat a cat, staring at us. Almost rudely, you'd have said. That afternoon we returned to the house where Nico's mother had lived, emboldened, no doubt, by our experience. It bucks you up, to think for a moment that scientific materialism might have a distant, eccentric cousin who occasionally turns up at the party and does tricks. Well, not tricks, no. Sings strange songs, maybe, or transfixes you with a wise look in a pair of tired and knowing eyes.

I am not going to start saying, at this late stage, that I believe in it all – the miracles, the signs in the sky, the portents and the tea leaves. And yet. And yet, always glad when I can find in a book something that dignifies my more aberrant thoughts, even if only by suggesting they might have poetic if not factual value, I was pleased to discover that Carl Jung himself had had an 'exploding knife' experience. His mother's young cousin Hélène was sixteen when she began to suffer from psychological disturbances which seemed to find their expression in physical events in the outside world. At the time, Jung was only twenty-four himself, and Hélène was probably in love with him, and he a little with her. Jung was trying to decide whether to specialise in surgery or 'internal medicine', and was profoundly affected by an incident that occurred during the summer holidays. From the dining room, where his mother sat knitting, came a noise like a pistol shot. The round table had split in two. It had been 'the dowry of my paternal grandmother'. It was not a hot day, he says, and the wood had not shown any signs of stress. His mother 'nodded darkly. "Yes, yes," she said, "that means something."' Two weeks later a similar loud bang was heard, from inside the heavy nineteenth-century sideboard. Inside the piece of furniture Jung found a loaf of bread and a breadknife beside it. The greater part of the blade had snapped in several pieces. The knife had been used shortly before, at four o'clock tea, and afterwards put away. Since then no one had gone to the sideboard. The following day Jung took the shattered pieces to 'one of the best cutlers in town', who declared that there was no fault in the steel and that someone must deliberately have broken it piece by piece. 'Good steel can't explode.'

Coming across an incident like this in a book, one thinks, Oh, one of those incidents, yes. But when it occurs, in your hand, with the accompanying noise and jolt up your arm, you don't immediately put it into a set of 'that kind of incident', you think, What on earth was that? It is extraordinary because it is unaccountable and contrary to the accepted laws of nature, mechanics and common sense. Particularly in the case of an exploding knife, where it is not merely a question of coincidence. If we had opened the local free newspaper and the son of the potter with whom Nico had hoped to do an apprenticeship fifty years earlier had been inviting people to come to an open workshop – as also happened – that would have been a coincidence. Or perhaps, Jung would suggest, a 'meaningful coincidence'. But what interaction of particles and energy could conceivably, in the gloom of a back-room bar, cause a knife to snap in two? Throughout his career as a writer and psychiatrist/analyst, Jung struggled with the paranormal. He hesitated to declare more than a scientific interest in it, for fear his colleagues and the world would dismiss him as a crank, and his serious work with patients on the psyche, dreams and memory be discredited, subject even to ridicule and scorn. Towards the end of his career, as often happens, he allowed himself greater freedom to speak of his beliefs, objecting to the empiricists' limiting way of 'forcing nature to give answers to questions devised by man'.

I told a friend once about Miss Moberly and Miss Jourdain and my fixation with them and their sightings in the garden of Versailles. Although he was French, he had never been to Versailles, and regarded my having visited the palace as a child as a typically English piece of eccentricity. 'And,' I added, 'when Miss Jourdain was a young girl, she had a repeating dream that she was in a long eighteenth-century gallery, and at the far end of the gallery there was a woman playing a harpsicord; it was always the same piece. And every time, before she got to the end of the piece, a servant came in and said something, and she got up and went out. After she had had the dream a few times, Miss Jourdain found she could play the piece when she woke up. Her mother wrote it down. Later they found out it was *"Les Barricades mysterieuses"* by Couperin! What do you think of that?' He laughed so loud that his dog woke up and he said, *'Je n'en pense rien!'* meaning not 'It's all nonsense' but 'I have no thoughts about it.' That thinking wasn't the point. I like the fact that whenever I start to dwell on ideas that seem resistant to Cartesian analysis and thought as such, I remember his laugh, which had no mockery in it, but was more of a joyful shout, like the release of a spring.

We haven't told the children the story of the exploding knife. Perhaps because it isn't really a story. It has no ending. Nothing changed as a result of the shattering of the knife, it wasn't symbolic of anything. It just made us feel that the current mechanistic view of the world, which doesn't allow for acausal events, might only be a partial view, as every other view in history has been, however state-of-the art. The flat declaration that we are lumbering robots, machines with genetically programmed brains, might be — as we all apprehend that it is, without knowing why, and not just because we want, among other things, to survive death — mistaken. We felt emboldened and more hopeful, like one of the children on their first visit to Narnia being given a silver quiver, or a potion in a tiny flask.

The cure for anything is salt water: sweat, tears or the sea.

Isak Dinesen, *Seven Gothic Tales*

For the first few months back in England Clara struggled. Verity was fine; she expected little and was pleasantly surprised. Clara was wary of other children. She was like a horse that has lost its confidence in people. Her form mistress had a daughter who also had cystic fibrosis, in her twenties, which should have been an advantage, but somehow seemed to make life harder for Clara. The form mistress understood. But to go from a situation where nobody understood to one where someone understood all too well was almost too much. I wish she'd stop talking about it, Clara said. We had to try and explain that people could be genuine, that she should not expect always to be hurt. She began to drop her guard. Then in May her lung function plummeted. I could hear her coming long before she entered the room, short wheezy breaths. Carrying her schoolbag became an effort. She lay in bed in the morning looking grey and exhausted, her lips chapped and sore, her hair lifeless. All the energy had gone out of her. The doctors in Bristol said she must come into hospital for two weeks and have intravenous antibiotics. This is part of the standard treatment for CF. The lung function drops below a certain percentage, and they pump you with antibiotics. Through a line the antibiotics get to where they need to be much faster than when taken orally. We dreaded the procedure, but were familiar with it, and were told it would fix her up.

She and I occupied a room on the top floor of the Bristol children's hospital. It was half-term week and then exam week. She made films of a seagull who sat outside her window. We watched *Blackadder* and *Miranda* all the way through on the iPad, and the nurses taught me and Nico to administer the intravenous drugs ourselves. That way when she needed IVs in future – it was anticipated that it would be increasingly necessary – we would be able to keep her at home, away from hospital bugs. We trained twice a day for ten days, under the watchful and infinitely patient eye of the nurses, making up the doses from powder and saline, drawing the saline out of plastic phials with a needle and syringe, injecting the saline into the powder, drawing the mixed solution back into a syringe, laying out up to ten syringes on a sterilised tray, attaching some of them to pumps so that they could be injected very slowly; each one went into the tube in her arm, over a period of an hour. Once we were judged competent we brought her home. She drew and read and made exquisite paper dresses for hand-high dolls. Where are her friends? I wondered. She had made a few friends, but didn't seem to feel secure with any of them. She found school dynamics bewildering, any sharp talk made her flinch. Although the girls knew about the CF, having been told all about it by the form mistress, they hadn't seemed to understand. They were in Year 7, all jostling for position, all anxious and unsure.

But after she returned from hospital everything changed. Four girls stepped forwards – in my mind I saw it as a horse-shoe shape, from which four girls stepped out and claimed her. She went back into school for the last Friday afternoon of the week and ran the 200-metre hurdles. She said she collapsed just short of the line, and one of the girls came and took her hand and ran the rest of the way. From that moment on, she was no longer alone. It took four girls plus Clara to make a world. Laughter filled the house, the phone rang, girls were everywhere, writing stories and songs, making cakes, drawing, playing tag, having sleepovers and listening to music. The person who stood to lose out was Verity, who had left her home and friends in France. She and Clara had always been like sisters in a nineteenth-century novel who spent every moment of their lives together. Perhaps she watched these new friendships warily, suspecting they might flare and fade. I began to get a glimpse of what life must be like in other families.

Clara's cough was still there, though. The treatment didn't seem to have worked. Her lung function was still 20 per cent down on what it had been even when we arrived in the UK.

I met a woman in the playground who had also been a novelist until she had a baby. We must have met before in London, because we were published on the same list. 'Do you still write?' 'I ghost-write,' she said, 'for the money. But mostly I work as a healer.' She came to visit Clara when she came out of hospital. Clara rose to meet her; she knew the moment she saw her, she said, that she was a healer, that she would help. In the barn of the new house, which Nico had made into a library, Clara lay on the sofa while Roz crouched beside her.

Roz said I could sit in with them if I liked, but I didn't want to, though I was just next door and could hear their voices. I knew that Clara was happy to trust people outside the family, that this tight cord that bound us needed to slacken. Roz used her hands, not to touch her physically, but just placing them above her lungs. 'What do you feel?'

'It's warm,' Clara said.

'And is it getting warmer or cooler?'

'It's getting warmer and warmer.'

'Can you see anything? With your eyes closed?'

'Red . . . orange now; it's getting hotter.' There was a flash, she said, an '*éclair*'. Then it was too hot, and she asked Roz to stop. Roz's hands moved down her body, drawing the heat down to the ground. Clara slept for three hours. I don't think she had ever slept for three hours in the day, not even when she was a baby. Afterwards she felt warm and peaceful. Roz said she made no claims for what she did, but that she was convinced that the energy passing through her to Clara could make her stronger, help her to heal herself.

Nostalgia is always barren. There is no risk in it, but it will not surprise you either. I am always prepared to stand up for the possibility of growth through change, stress, error and mishap. It's in my genes. It's a feature of sexual reproduction, it's what makes us human. I don't think one should assume that being human is necessarily an achievement in itself, but as opportunities go, it beats being a mushroom or a bacterial cell. In the summer holidays we returned to France to empty the house, but everything was faded and there was not much pleasure in it. The thing had stopped growing. It was like going out with someone you've dramatically and supposedly definitely broken up with, for a further couple of weeks, with due stages of elation, poignant regret and finally exasperation and confirmation of the opinion that originally made you split up. On this trip Clara was so allergic to everything that we had to get the dog out of the house in case she was responsible. Clara's lips were red and raw, her face blotchy and taut. When she woke up in the morning she felt ragged and tearful with exhaustion. I rang a friend and said, 'Can you take Posy? Now? I don't know how long for. For ever, maybe?' and she said, 'OK.'

Sometimes kindness can be a bold piece of action, not just a mild disposition of the heart. I'd known Marianne for years. One summer we gave a concert in a beautiful church about three kilometres from our village. Some people sat in deck-chairs. It was a very strange programme. I played two pieces by Percy Grainger, about whom one could write an entire memoir, to include mention of his collection of whips, his penchant for complex arrangements of simple folk tunes and his unerring fidelity to his Australian mother. One was 'Country Gardens', and the other, towards the end of the programme, 'Danny Boy'. I hate speaking in public, but I did then, because I wanted to say that I was playing it for my mother, who couldn't be there because she was in a residential care home in Nottinghamshire. Marianne chose two pieces to sing – without knowing they were pieces we particularly loved; one was 'Donna Donna' by Joan Baez, which we often sang in the car, and the other was *'Lascia ch' io Pianga'*, which I had listened to over and over when Clara was first diagnosed. After she had sung the second piece she came over to the piano, kissed me and said, 'That was for you.' Nico said that he had never known such straightforward love as he encountered between women. I used to think women who cultivated and celebrated their female friendships were just making the best of a bad job, but now I regret wasting so much of my life on self-seeking relationships with men whom I could never love and who were wasting their time trying to love me. Or should that be the other way round? Marianne now says that Posy was the best gift anyone ever gave her, and I felt she had given us the best possible gift in return, making Posy a beautiful home on a farm, with horses and a pond.

~

The children slept over at Sabine's one night, in a tent. The river flows through their farm, and the next day they paddled. Clara had been told not to go into the river this summer; the level was low and it bred bacteria. She agreed just to paddle. But the others called to her to wade out to where the water was deeper and faster, and she could feel her feet losing their grip on the stones and the tug of the water on her body, which was so slight, a tiny reed. She began to panic, convinced she was about to be swept off her feet. She could swim well, but was frightened she would swallow water and catch pseudomonas again. And it wasn't an unreasonable fear. Verity took her by the hand, waded back to the shore with her and sat with her on the bank till she stopped shaking. 'I had to explain to Verity,' Sabine said, 'that she is a separate person to her sister. She does not have the illness. She needs to remember that.'

Hanging over us all that summer was the thought that Clara had her annual hospital review in Bristol in mid-August. I knew her lung function would be down, and the tests would probably reveal further decline, weight loss, digestive deficiency and actual lung damage, seen in scarring on the X-ray. In France they had said they didn't like to X-ray annually because the anticipation was that children of Clara's age with CF would live a long time, and they were wary of exposing them to too much radiation. Now the doctors didn't seem so concerned about the long term, they felt keeping an eye on her lung damage was too important to worry about the risk.

I was so anxious, Nico took her. I felt my presence made it harder for her sometimes. He was calm and orderly and kept her in relatively good humour. But hospital makes children grouchy and raw, and sometimes their mothers too.

When they got home, Nico said: 'They want her to go on the trial.' Her results had not been too bad, but her lung function was low enough for her to qualify.

Everyone knew about Kalydeco. When Clara was a baby the great hope was the Gene Therapy Consortium, a research group uniting labs in Edinburgh, Oxford and London. They are still having difficulty finding a way to introduce the corrected gene without the body rejecting it. In the meantime, a company in America had been working on a drug that basically acts to stop the body overproducing mucus. If the mucus is no longer produced – as a reaction to the faulty transmission of salt molecules in the CF-affected organism – there is nowhere for infection to breed. The conditions in which the bacteria thrive simply vanish. That was the theory. In 2013 it became apparent that, for a small percentage (4) of the CF population who have a particular mutation called G551D, a drug was now ready for use that did just this.

There are two possible problems in CF. One is that your sodium chloride (salt) molecules can't pass from one cell to the next because the 'gate' between the cells is sealed shut. And the other is that even if the gate were open, the salt molecules wouldn't be able to get through because they are folded in on themselves, and need to be opened up. People with Clara's mutation have the folding and the gating problem. People with G551D only have the gating problem. Kalydeco opens the gate.

Reports began to appear on the internet of people who had had CF all their lives, many of them on the lung transplant waiting list, whose lung function was soaring overnight from 30 per cent to the 70s and above, who were suddenly gaining weight. Their blogs made incredible reading. I always felt guilty reading up about CF on the internet. It felt like a vice, and I did it usually after dark, when the rest of the family was sleeping. The doctors discouraged us from reading too much. They wanted parents and patients to focus on the everyday tasks of airway clearance, nutrition, exercise, nebulisers, drugs. They believed that if families placed too much confidence in the drugs of the future they would neglect to do the simple but vital things that kept their children's lungs in reasonable condition (by CF standards), the hope of a pharmaceutical fix would compromise the commitment to care. So even though I knew Kalydeco existed, and I knew also that trials were going on of a combined therapy, Kalydeco plus a second drug which aimed to tackle the disease in patients with Clara's gene mutation, I didn't allow the thought of it to do much more than just slightly take the edge off the pain I felt when I thought about the future.

We made little use of the future tense. Occasionally we said 'if there's a cure'. When we stirred the Christmas cake in France, with neighbours and friends all sitting round an enormous African bowl on the kitchen table, with a paddle of a wooden spoon, I was always pretty sure everyone was making the same wish. When we blew out birthday-cake candles too.

When Clara was two and a half, though, a team from the BBC came to the house to film her. They were making a short film about cystic fibrosis as part of a Sunday-evening charity appeal. The producer had thought out her questions carefully in advance. On the phone, preparing the interview we'd do for the camera, she'd said, 'I imagine birthdays are rather bittersweet in your household.' I didn't at first grasp what she meant. It was true that Nico was an elderly father, that I sometimes felt the poignancy of his ageing, with these two very young daughters around. Though I think I worried more about them being teased for having an elderly father than about the possibility of his dying while they were still young. But what she meant was that Clara's relatively short life expectancy must lend poignancy to each of her birthdays. Each one brought her nearer to an early death. I had never thought of this before, and I can't say I was grateful to her for drawing it to my attention. And to emphasise the insight, they brought a birthday cake round to the flat and asked her to blow out the candles while they filmed. There were only three then. With each year, as we put another candle on the cake, I feel a sense of achievement, that we have brought her through another year; of pride, that she's managed, with the lungs she has, to blow out the candles in one go; and a flicker of uncertainty and fear as I remember the producer's words.

In the film they also featured a young woman called Nicky, who must have been in her mid-twenties. I remember she was beautiful, with a cracked voice and a smile that was strangely reassuring, considering that she knew she didn't have long to live. Around that time she and her – now late – friend Alice Martineau, a model and singer of around the same age (to name only two people, but there are hundreds; I noticed them because they were English, and they were daughters), both inspired fund-raising efforts that have made an incalculable difference to the children in the generation following theirs. Without the fund-raising of supporters over the years, Kalydeco would never have been developed. No one would know the location of the CF gene (on chromosome 7), the malfunction would not have been understood, and the chemical capable of correcting it would not have been isolated.

When Clara ran five kilometres recently in aid of the Cystic Fibrosis Trust, one boy in her year said his father had told him not to sponsor her, because he believed that he paid his taxes to fund a health service, and that charities shouldn't be fund-raising for medical care. I understood his point of view. But it was really those small, accumulated sums of money that came from cake sales and sponsored runs that brought Kalydeco to development stage. Acts of love. Plus a kind of mad faith on the part of a handful of inspired scientists. Fortunately, the CF fix became the obsession of a few scientists who happened to be facing in the right direction when the wind blew. That's the only way I can think of it. The chances of this drug reaching the stage it has reached, as far as my daughter's bloodstream, were incredibly remote. That she should have been born at the right time, lived in the right place – the chances of all this happening were slight beyond all reasonable hope.

The mention of the six-month trial threw open all the windows of hope I had never dared even look out of, let alone unlatch. Though it meant many hospital visits, an increase in the number of pills she had to take each day, the possibility of side-effects, the one-in-three chance she would only be on the placebo, the one-in three-chance she would only be on the gate-opening drug, and the one-in-three chance that she would be on the gate-opening *and* the unfolding drug. We asked her if she wanted to do it. She wasn't sure.

We dithered for a few days, a couple of weeks maybe, and then we all decided at once that we couldn't not do it. I read a post on the internet by a woman saying she would move states, sell her house, change jobs, if it meant she could get her daughter on the trial. We rang the hospital and said

Clara would take part. They were recruiting 501 children in Australia, Europe and certain other countries. We all went to the hospital one day in late August, when they explained to her what it involved, what a placebo was, how the results were gathered, though not what results they expected to see. Nobody said, 'This may change your life.' I was touched to see the doctor and Clara studying the papers together, trying to work out the programme of the trial. For the first time ever, she didn't feel like a patient, but a collaborator. Verity sat listening to *The Hitchhiker's Guide to the Galaxy* on the iPad and taking the occasional photo. They rang the next day, to say she would start two days after she went back to school. They called it Day 1. And it seemed she would be the only person on the trial in the south-west of England. Other people had been invited, but she had been the first to accept and be screened, and the day after she was signed up, the company conducting the trial closed the lists. She was Child 501.

Because every aspect of the trial was conducted with the utmost rigour, it seemed all the more surprising that so much emphasis was placed on the possibility of a placebo effect. Though Clara appeared to be better almost immediately, the doctor said it was quite possible that the improvement in her lung function and general well-being was due to her belief that she was taking pills that could cure her – even if they were actually just pink tablets made of entirely inert substances, of purely symbolic value. This seems to be the only area in which mainstream medicine allows magical thinking to peep its head round the door.

~

I felt sure after a couple of days that she wasn't on the placebo. Although she was underweight, she had always felt heavy, with, I think it is not fanciful to say, a great psychological weight. Suddenly she felt light. Where once trying to clear her lungs felt like squeezing a bottle of washing-up liquid, now it reminded me more of blowing down a penny whistle. There was no resistance. The laws of nature hadn't been modified or overturned. But thanks to the brilliance and dedication of a small number of researchers, a channel had opened, allowing water and salt to begin to flow.

'You didn't deserve this,' my cousin had said, and I secretly thought that I probably had, but Clara most definitely hadn't, so deserving probably didn't come into it. But after a year in England, I really felt 'I didn't deserve this.' I never expected, let alone deserved, such a gift.

Endings and beginnings . . . our own beginnings and our own endings are in themselves stories, all tangled with the beginnings and endings of other stories. It is the writer's job to find an ending, perhaps to decide just which ending from several possible endings is the correct one to present in print – to externalise – for after the choice is made the ending seems inevitable and *true*, categorical rather than contingent.

Margaret Mahy, *A Dissolving Ghost*

Clara wanted to give a friend a special birthday present. On the beach she met a man fishing for mackerel. He caught several within minutes of each other, put them in a bucket and gave them to her. When we'd cooked the fish and eaten it, Clara boiled up the seawater from the bucket until nothing but salt was left. She put the salt in a jar with a screw-top lid and gave it to her friend. The friend came to stay but she forgot the jar when she packed. For a few months it sat on the shelf in Clara's room. Eventually she took a spoonful of the salt and put it into a loaf of bread she was making for a school friend who had just moved house. She'd heard that when someone moved house you should give them bread and salt. Together they sprinkled some of the salt on the ledge of her bedroom window, saved the rest for baking, and ate the bread.

Gifts should flow from one person to another. The quotations in this book were all taken from underlinings in books on my desk or, in some cases, poems the children had learned at school, words that had arrived uninvited and then resonated, made greater sense of things, and that I wanted to pass on. Thinking about the sodium chloride, unable to pass from cell to cell, causing all that disturbance in a body, reinforced my sense that to keep things flowing was important. We all have our private myths, metaphors that remind us how to live, which we build into the stories we tell and the stories our own lives tell. 'Let your life speak,' the Quakers say.

In the school the children go to now there are pupils from many different backgrounds and nationalities. Bonded members of social groups have particular ways of communicating, not all of which we understand. In the great murmurations of starlings over the Somerset Levels near Glastonbury, at Ham Wall and Shapwick Heath, millions of birds swirl and swoop, unchoreographed and faultless against the smoky blue sky at dawn and dusk. Each one an individual, each with parent birds, each family part of a flock, each sensitive to the slightest movement of all the others, harmony without baton or constraint. It is an incomprehensible glory, but it is not ours. Our instincts are more varied and divergent and our forms of co-operation more laboriously learned. We need our narratives and models to guide us; some invented and others true.

It is good that an account of the past, an account of anything really, can be – should be – selective. There is something very pleasant and easeful about skipping certain things, deciding not to write about them yet, or ever, letting them slide. I am just writing some selected things down, not all of it, not even the most important things necessarily, because if I don't they will sit there like the water on the Somerset Levels, unable to drain away.

Writing as drainage. I can still remember sitting in the car, looking out across the Lincolnshire fields towards the sea, waiting for my father to emerge from a Methodist chapel where he would have been conducting the Sunday-morning 'act of worship', with my mother describing how Cornelius Vermuyden drained the land in the seventeenth century and rendered it fertile and brought prosperity to the people of Lincolnshire. The village where we lived, where my father would have been preaching, was, like the village in France, like the village we have moved to in Somerset, a medieval inland port, a place of silt and flow, and rich alluvium.

We unconsciously repeat our choices – but to what end? Is it a process, a working through, or a purely decorative, unreflective pattern? A man has published a book about cases he has dealt with in psychoanalysis. He says we can lead hideously contorted lives simply in order not to recognise a truth about something, that we will go to incredible lengths in order not to recognise or accept change, because change entails loss and we can't accept loss. Am I repeating any patterns in order not to acknowledge painful loss?

Have I truly accepted my mother's death? With each anniversary we will repeat a little the day of her death, but there is a process of forgetting, too. Sometimes when people with dementia die, relatives say they consider the first, real loss took place earlier, before they died. I tried not to think this. (Alain Mabanckou's mother died in the Congo after he moved to live in France, when he hadn't seen her for seven years, and for more than a decade after her death he pretended to the outside world that she was still alive.) I sang to her the last time I saw her, Methodist hymns at first, then, when they drew no response, 'What shall we do with the drunken sailor?', at which she laughed and squeezed my hand and said, 'Nice singing.' She was not lost to me then. Am I frantically anxious about Clara because of something to do with my mother? People said to me when she was a baby, in shops, 'Ah, enjoy it, they grow up so quickly,' but they also said, 'You've got a job for life there.' It is said that the day your first child is born is when the worry starts. But I don't worry about Verity, not in the same way, and I wonder whether people who have children who don't have an illness feel about their children as I do about Verity, a love which is, so far, without difficulty, tension or anxiety. If Clara is ever cured, will I leap free of this anxiety? It seems unlikely, it has become such a habit of mind. (Verity said to me the other day, 'What is peace of mind?' and I said, 'When you just accept whatever happens and are calm,' and she said, 'Like Papa?')

In Somerset the children and I joined the parish-church choir, which rehearses at the end of the week, on a Friday evening, when everything else is done. The fifteenth-century church is spacious and light, and their voices resonate beautifully off the stone. I stand opposite them, none of us believers, but here anyway, for the music, again, and for the things we might feel if we truly did believe. I love to look over at them as they sing, so unconsciously, with the relaxed kind of concentration child choristers often have, inwardly fashioning something which emerges without fuss or apparent effort, complex and ready-made. One week we sang a beautiful piece of music by Eleanor Daley, which I had never heard before. The words are from the 'Song of Solomon':

> Set me as a seal upon your heart, as a seal upon
> your arm.
> For love is strong as death.
> Many waters cannot quench love. Neither can the
> floods drown it.
> For love is strong as death.

While we sang, a large brown butterfly drew erratic patterns high up in the vault over our heads, and the children, noticing it, grinned across at me. Remembering, with the girls, how the woman at my mother's funeral had said, 'Did you see the butterfly?', I thought nothing, and everything, of it. Primo Levi talks about the attractiveness to us of butterflies, saying, 'We would not think them so beautiful if they did not fly, or if they flew straight and briskly like bees, or if they stung, or above all if they did not enact the perturbing mystery of meta-morphosis.' He describes what emerges from the cocoon as 'a psyche, a soul, and the ripped open cocoon, which is left on the ground, is the mortal remains'. When we got to the words 'For love is strong as death', the butterfly swooped down and sat on the left of my chest, where I would lay my hand if you asked me where my heart was. It stayed there for the rest of the choir practice. Like a seal upon my heart.

It is easy to draw a meaning from what happened. It is always too easy, really, to draw lessons from things. As the daughter of a preacher I am all too prone to it, though in my case it blurs with a kind of superstition that says, 'And that was a bit weird, because . . . ' But if we hadn't left France and given up the life we had built there, because Clara was being bullied at school, we would never be here now, with Clara sleeping upstairs, breathing easily, her lungs clear, the tension gone from her features, messages from friends stacking up on her phone, a hint of weight gain, a new sense of possibility in our lives. We still think of the time we spent there; in a way we sold our life in France quite cheaply, on a hunch, and were rewarded a thousandfold – more. But nothing is assured. There are days when Clara is less well. She still has the same regime of hospital visits, medication and occasional admissions, but there is hope that she will live as long as other people, that her life will not be one of pain, struggle and decline towards an early death. Now they are talking about gene therapy again, and trials are already taking place to see whether it is possible actually to introduce a normal version of the gene into the body, to issue better instructions.

While we were in France, I read a review in an English newspaper of a television programme in which a student with cystic fibrosis – that is to say, with ten years or so to go, with decreasing quality of life, before she might expect to die of lung disease – went to interview the researchers developing the gene therapy that might throw the switch and turn on the lights that were gradually shutting down inside her body. I didn't see the programme, but the review was quite encouraging. The reviewer ended up by saying that the unspoken subtext to the film, which was on the whole very optimistic about the generation of drugs currently being developed, was a polite 'Get a bloody move on!' And they have.

Gene therapy had always been – is still – medicine's brightest hope. I often thought of the health worker crossing herself when I told her Clara was being tested for cystic fibrosis and whispering, 'Please God, not that, not *that*.' She'd recovered, and said of course now there were lung transplants, heart transplants. And gene therapy, I'd said, because I'd been told it was in the pipeline, and she'd given me a superstitious look, as though I had a lamp in my pocket that I might whip out and polish at any moment. I suppose she thought I meant 'genie' therapy. That would be nice, too.

There are two kinds of gene therapy, somatic and germline. Somatic therapy sends in a corrected version of the faulty gene on a retrovirus, which then goes round placing the corrected version of the gene in all the billions of cells in our bodies, like a lamp lighter going down the street igniting each lamp at sunset. Germline therapy corrects the gene on the chromosome in the sex cell, so that not only is the fault corrected in the person with an illness – Parkinson's, sickle cell disease, potentially Alzheimer's and cancer too – but their offspring and all subsequent generations will also have a healthy copy of the gene, a copy that will give rise to good health in the carrier. Most people now agree that somatic gene therapy for people with genetically carried illnesses is desirable and beneficial. If they don't now they probably will by the time they or their children are in a position to benefit from such developments. We conserve our ancient – and perhaps justifiably reactionary – instincts for germline therapy.

The GM debate is especially heated in England. Mary Shelley gave us Frankenstein's monster, which has become part of our emotional architecture; and in the 1990s, the mad-cow crisis put the whole population on the alert against practices that are perceived as 'unnatural' – in that case, the feeding of contaminated animal products to cows and the resulting havoc in the brains of young burger consumers. At the school where my father worked, several pupils and former pupils were said to have died of it. An ancient taboo against species eating their own had been broken. A mistake that invites the wrath of the gods is one way of seeing it. Maybe the ancient gods understood their genetics perfectly well but decided it was rather complicated for us, and chose to explain it in stories about taboos and the disastrous consequences of disobedience.

Gene therapy is coming over the horizon. It's nearly here; and cystic fibrosis fortunately attracts the attentions of scientists. The short life expectancy of people who have CF lends an urgency to the quest. Children born at the turn of the century, if they get gene therapy, may meet or exceed present life expectancies for healthy people. The Gene Therapy Consortium led by Professor Eric Alton has been looking for a way to make gene therapy work for people with cystic fibrosis since 1997.

One of the things that struck me as significant about the work of Professor Alton and his team from the outset was its collaborative nature. For decades, university departments all over the world had been competing to crack the gene-therapy nut. Thousands and thousands of hours and huge sums of money were wasted in the replication of research. It was known that the corrected gene could effect the required change in the body. The difficulty was finding a way in. The two possible ways of introducing the corrected version of the gene are on a liposome or a virus, and I imagined these as two different kinds of flying dragon. The virus turned out to create problems for the person, giving them flu-like symptoms. Liposomes now seem to work better, and Professor Alton's recent trials used them. But already they are looking at a virus that has been isolated, out of hundreds and hundreds of thousands, that doesn't harm the host person, and which will bring in the gene more effectively. Combine that with the protein therapy Clara is on at the moment, to open the gate, and the expectation is that the ability of the corrected gene to maintain its position will be still further enhanced.

Right from the start, when the woman who worked for the Cystic Fibrosis Trust looked me in the eye and said, 'She's going to be OK,' and I decided to believe her, I prayed that Professor Alton wouldn't be killed in an air crash or sucked out to sea by a rip-tide while on holiday with his family. When a bomb exploded in Tavistock Square on 7 July 2005, he could easily have been on his way in to a meeting at the BMA. At the same time I knew that because he had drawn so many people into his research team, from different, incidentally not-for-profit academic institutions, his work was built on solid foundations, its base was broad and stable. In *The Gift* Lewis Hyde describes the ideal community of academic scientists as a 'gift-sharing community'. The gifts are the ideas, and they circulate freely. It is a complex area and is set to grow more complex as the ideas get closer to finding a material expression, in the form of pharmaceuticals which have to be manufactured, bought, sold and consumed. That this extraordinary scientific progress should occur in Clara's generation – and yours, and your children's – feels even more unbelievably statistically unlikely than that she should be born with the gene in the first place. Children with cystic fibrosis of her generation are likely to be the lucky ones.

In May 2015, fifteen years after the creation of the GTC, Eric Alton walked into one of those rather old-fashioned auditoriums in Imperial College, looking for all the world as though he'd just chained his bike to a drainpipe outside and stuffed his cycle clips into his pocket, and talked to an invited audience of parents and CF doctors about the progress they had made. Interested parties had been alerted by email to the live streaming of the event. It was a beautiful day in May. In Somerset, Clara and Verity were outside bouncing on the trampoline. I could hear them laughing and calling to each other, their voices exaggeratedly high with the exertion. Nico and I sat on the sofa watching the presentation of the results on a laptop, live. Yes, said the professor, we have the results of trials, and they are a modest success. He explained how they could be improved on. No one was cheering, no lights were flashing, but I felt that I was watching something momentous, a scientist who had worked for the greater part of his professional life to be able to say quietly, 'We have a modest success.' Nobody felt disappointed. It was the beginning of something. 'Is it good?' Clara asked as she came through on her way to the kitchen for a glass of water. Nico nodded.

That night Clara said, 'I don't want gene therapy. I don't want them to take my CF away. It's part of who I am. If they take it away I won't be me any more. Can't they just take the symptoms away, but I get to keep the gene?'

'Anything that takes the symptoms away has to be repeated over and over. Gene therapy might eventually just work once and for all.'

'But I wouldn't mind, if it was once a week, or once a month.' As though it could be like going to Mass, or the gym. To maintain one's well-being through observance might be a healthy way to live, remaining mindful of one's good fortune and not taking it for granted. Clara had a sense that her identity was bound up with her CF, both the identity she'd been born with and the identity she'd forged for herself, living with it all these years. Now she was worrying that without the gene she'd lose something of that.

People with cystic fibrosis never meet. Clara and Jack met once in a corridor in the hospital in Toulouse, and they were both — in accordance with hygiene rules in French hospitals that don't obtain in the UK — wearing mouth masks, so only their eyes met. I felt as though they were hostages being kept prisoner in different parts of a building, whose paths had accidentally crossed. They hadn't spoken, but they now knew that it was true the other — and therefore a whole host of others — existed. And Clara had never expressed a wish to be part of a cystic fibrosis community, though there are online forums now, and virtual friendships are beginning to develop; but you can't rub shoulders with another person with CF. You can't invite them to a party or go out for a meal with them, or on holiday. In Clara's case, and it was a case that was accentuated by our living in France, where already we were 'other' to some degree, her identity never came from being part of a group. As the older child she at first existed in a set of one. Verity was a carrier, an ensign bearer, on the field but ultimately *hors de combat*. And this singularity has become one of Clara's defining characteristics. In her tastes, her enthusiasms, her chosen activities, she seems to be naturally singular; though she often operates in a cluster, it's usually with friends who are similarly singular. When she came out of hospital that first time, and found herself the object of bullying in the playground, she refused to make the slightest concession, to get the One Direction pencil case, say, for a quiet life. She suffered because she fought for her own identity, but she also survived because she fought for it. It's not surprising, then, that she should worry about a doctor taking it away.

It was not from her that I learned that between mothers and daughters there exists an immutable and rigid love called the sacred, which cannot be broken except at the price of curses and scandal. On the contrary, she detached me, she shook me free with an imperious hand.

Colette, on her mother, Sido, En Pays Connu

It was a lovely house, and the garden was lovely, and when Clara asked Nico what he would miss most about being there after we left, he said without hesitation, 'The night sky and the walls.' I would have said I would miss the happiness I felt when I closed the shutters at night and looked out at the garden, particularly the front garden, in May and early June, when the roses were indescribably beautiful and the broad paddle leaves on the fig tree were new in, and you could already catch the smell of the fruit to come, just from the leaves when they'd been in the sun but weren't dried out by the full summer heat. It isn't that I will miss the roses, but that I will miss the happiness they brought me. I won't miss the town, but I will miss the joy of the years we spent there. What will the children miss most? I think they will probably remember, at least, a feeling they had on a Wednesday morning, when I had already gone out to work, as they left the house by the back door and walked up the alley, with tall medieval buildings blocking out most of the light, stopping, in the summer, to pop the seed pods of the *impatiens*, and crossing the street opposite the *mairie*, up into the church square to the presbytery where the priest might be on his knees or up a ladder or playing football, for catechism. They often moaned about going, but they met their friends there and always came back singing and laughing, with other girls in tow. Nico would cycle up to the pizza van on the market and order enough for everyone and I would come home after six hours of teaching piano and eat up the remains of lunch while the little girls drew and painted with Françoise. I hope they remember that and not the other things. The house will be sold and they will walk past it, if they do return, and be surprised at the colour of the shutters, and marvel at the height of the climbing rose I bought for Nico's birthday the first autumn we lived there. I dream that one of them will buy the house back one day. Or maybe I will, though I can't imagine any of us will be able to afford it.

Nico says, 'Never go back.' I met a man at a party the other evening who said he had been on a retreat in the Sinai Desert and on the first day he said, 'Well, God, what do you have in mind for me?' and got no answer. On the second day he asked the same question, but again received no answer. 'On the third day,' he said, 'I asked the question again and a voice' – in his own head – 'said, "Go back!"' He said that when he started looking into it there were lots of people in the Bible to whom God had said, 'Go back!' I wondered if God hadn't also added, 'And stop asking me the same question every day. There *is* no plan!' So far I haven't gone back to anywhere I've lived before, and though I have not quite moved around enough to be running out of places, it sometimes feels like it.

When we left the house and moved to Somerset, where it rained, and the vegetables on the market were all purple, or huge and bulging, from entirely respectable natural causes, I wrote to friends I had left behind that I felt we needed to grow new tissue. I can still gauge, somehow, though I could not put a measurement on it, the time it will take for the tissue to heal. I know worse things happen than leaving a house. People have said to me gallantly that, after death and divorce, moving house is the most traumatic thing you can experience. It's not true: illness is far worse, the deep unhappiness of one's child, and war, and poverty. I only allow myself to write about this particular, unremarkable form of loss because it is *our* loss, and to write about it might help us find the shape of the thing we have lost, like that shape of the absence in the bed. I have said to myself that it is not a rupture, not a severance, but a displacement, literally a removal, that the thing that is missing, and so much missed, will continue to exist in our absence. Sometimes, since we have friends there, we will even revisit. But it's the things we did there, the subjective, unrepeatable experiences, the essential breath of life, which is, as the priest tells us, as if we didn't know it, love. But the priest also says, though he is very young and perhaps would say something different if he were older, 'We can't change the past. The future's in the Lord's hands, so we'd better live today with all the love we have, and all our strength.'

In her essay on 'Motherhood Today', Julia Kristeva describes the process of gestation, expulsion, weaning, release and eventual detachment as the 'miracle of maternal passion' which, she says, 'while being the prototype of passion is also the prototype of letting go of passion'. It is a process that occurs slowly and in which the teaching of language to the child plays a crucial role. The language-learning process that initially takes place largely between the mother and the infant is full of mimickings and cooings and repetitions, by means of which the mother nudges the child towards naming, and eventually self-expression. These repeated sounds are called, deliciously, *echolalia*. Having your language and using it to make your own ideas and eventually tell your own stories: this is the envelope freedom comes in. And freedom, she says, is not so much the freedom to transgress the law, the father's edict and authority, but the freedom to begin again, to start anew, to not stagnate or atrophy. 'The marvel felt experiencing the ephemeral as a new beginning' overrides the angst we feel over 'the ephemeral nature of this life we, as mothers, have given'. It is a mother's capacity to sublimate her passion for her children that will make it possible for them to begin themselves to be creative and free.

There is much replication in a family. We pass on our genes, our traditions, our neuroses sometimes, our tastes, enthusiasms, prejudices, and our stories. I think of my mother embroidering, weaving, unravelling and restitching stories, and I know I must make my choices from what has been given to me. I shan't go and fetch a story from the other end of the world and try it on to see if it fits, returning it for a refund if it doesn't. I will try to experiment with what is in my closet, with my inheritance. This is an inheritance known to me only, and it is mine to invest or squander. My mother once observed that she had possibly 'over-invested' in her children, and I was appalled by the phrase, as though we were stocks and shares that might or might not yield a profit. The more you give away, with children, the more you have. There is a liberating paradox in that. But their lives and stories still grow from the old stock, and flourish, if they are able to thrive and become fertile, because in what we've passed on there's a little mixing up, and mistranslating, and meeting up and merging with the new. As with those altered *mise-en-abîme* pictures which are like but unlike, there is growth and change, not just replication.

For a mother to be able to embark on that journey of de-passioning – and it is not a journey over the course of which her love for her child decreases, far from it – she must somehow have regained the social world, have reconnected with her friends, her work, her other passions. During the year of my mother's death, when I began again to make music with other people, particularly women, I remembered what flowering of generosity and love can occur through a shared and sincere commitment to something greater than one-self, in which one has no 'investment'. Douglas Hofstadter says: 'What seems to be the epitome of selfhood, a sense of I, is in reality brought into being if and only if along with that self there is a sense of other selves with whom one has bonds of affection. In short only when generosity is born is an ego born.' Music, in this case the slow, long, finicky and difficult process of learning to make appear simple what was difficult – the rendering of Pergolesi's representation of one mother's pain, and the growth of suffering into hope – was the element through which I would rediscover that gener-osity and begin again to thrive. Possibly even, one day, to make stories.

Among the thousands of books in the house in France was *A Lion in the Meadow*, inherited from Nico's older chil-dren. It was first published in 1969, probably as a book to be read aloud to children not yet reading for themselves. The palette from which the colours were taken – the mother's dress, a pert, boldly patterned A shape, the lion itself, the late-summer grasses in the meadow – was dominated by mustard and orange shades. A little boy, sent out to play, complains to his mother that there's a lion in the meadow. Nonsense, says the mother, brusquely. The little boy adds an adjective and says there is a *yellow* lion in the meadow. Still she won't believe him, so he adds that the lion is 'big' and 'whiskery' and 'roaring'. There is nothing in the meadow but grass and trees, says the mother. He should go back and check. But he won't go back, he's too scared of the lion. See, says the mother, you're making up stories again. As though his unwillingness to go was proof of that, rather than the opposite. She takes the little boy on her knee. Since he is making up stories, she will make one up too. She gives him a matchbox and tells him that inside is a tiny dragon. If he opens the box the dragon will grow large and scare the lion away. The boy takes the matchbox. Their paths diverge. The boy goes into storyland; Mother goes on peeling potatoes. Then the door suddenly opens and the lion dashes in, terrified, looking for a place to hide from the dragon. The boy comes back in. 'There is a DRAGON in the meadow.' The mother tries to calm things down. 'There wasn't a real dragon. It was just a story I made up.' 'It turned out to be true after all,' says the little boy. 'You should have looked in the matchbox first.' It is the lion who says: 'That it is how it is. Some stories are true and some aren't.'

I couldn't find the original copy of the book against which to check my memory of the story, so I downloaded it on the Kindle instead and discovered that Margaret Mahy rewrote the ending in 1976. Our version ends with the words 'and the mother never, ever, made up a story again', which seemed like a terrible, fatal ending, the end of story-telling, the end of childhood, of fiction, of make-believe. The cost of make-believe was too high; the mother puts away her purse. In the newer, less punitive version, the dragon stayed in his meadow 'and nobody minded', and the lion in the meadow became a house lion and lived in the broom cupboard. In this rewrite, the sting in this tale has been removed. But every tale should have its sting, and this story hinges, it seems to me, on whether the mother continues to tell stories, and on the possibility that those stories just might turn out to be true. And stories that turn out to be true do so not by coincidence, but because the storyteller possesses some magic which brings stories into real life.

'Tea's ready!' I heard Verity tell Clara one day when they were playing a make-believe game.

'In the game or real life?' asked Clara.

'Um,' Verity said, popping her head round the kitchen door to check. She squinted at me.

'Real life,' she said. 'I *think*.'

Alors? ask our French friends. *Alors?*

I say, it's fine. No, it's good. Life's good. I pause, and then I say, it's not like before. It doesn't have the same – poetry, I guess. Is that because the children are older now? Because we are less frantic with worry, from day to day? Because the particular acute pain of my mother's death has transmuted into something more like a cheerless piece of general knowledge – that even your mother dies, in case you ever made believe to yourself she wouldn't? Or is the absence of poetry really due to the absence of music? When we were rehearsing the *Stabat Mater* I remember saying to the other two that silence in music could be of many different kinds. There is the silence of anticipation. The silence of desolation. The silence of peace. The silence of exhaustion. A replete silence, of contentment. The silence of surprise.

The summer after Clara started on the new treatment, we were in France, at my cousin's house. Beth and I walked round to the neighbour's garden to pick tomatoes. We could hear the children playing with the dogs back on the other side of the river. We no longer policed their every move for fear they'd drown in the reedy shallows at the end of the garden. It was a relief to walk away and know they could keep themselves safe. We had shared so many hours of keeping those flames alive, particularly Clara's, that it was a habit that required conscious effort to break. These moments were precious to us both. We never seemed to get enough time together, particularly now we lived in different countries. She had always sustained me, making me laugh, being angry on my behalf, loving my children so much that it made me less fearful of the possibility of my own death, or Nico's, or both. We seemed always to have our talks over the washing-up, or cooking, or on car journeys when everyone else was asleep, or even in the garden at family funerals, tight, hasty conversations in which many things were elided, because there wasn't time to state what we both knew. While we picked tomatoes we talked about the situation in Israel, which during that week was particularly violent. I had been in the car with the children on 12 June when an item came on the news about the kidnapping of three teenage Israeli soldiers, and the absurdity – always – of hearing about these distant events and having the very human capacity to imaginatively, for a moment, project oneself into the here-and-now of their occurrence, made me grip the steering wheel. 'Is it bad?' Clara asked. A telephone call had been made by one of the teenagers to a police hotline, reporting their kidnap, in a whisper. The whisper was followed by the sound of automatic gunfire.

My cousin said, as we picked the tomatoes, 'You've never been that interested in the outside world, have you?' She didn't mean it critically; she had just observed that compared to her family, ours was less news-conscious, less politically aware. I had been brought up in a house to which the *Daily Telegraph* was delivered before we woke, so that there was never a time, even in the early morning, when it wasn't there, stating its particular view of the case. I learned a lot of things that were never mentioned at table or in Sunday school from page 3 of the *Telegraph*. The pit village where my father was head of the comprehensive school was at the heart of the miners' strike and my father and Mrs Thatcher stood shoulder to shoulder to oppose it. It was a hellish time. I remember my mother telling me on the phone that she'd been standing at the kitchen sink peeling potatoes and could hear the clash of metal and the cries of men across the fields, as though she was having a flashback to Waterloo. My political education came from critically picking back over the incidents and discussions of my childhood, turning them all over and over to see them from different angles, realising their shape was not what I had perceived at the time.

The world changed for me when I became a mother. Suddenly it was much easier to be good! It was like being a child again: you knew what you had to do, and you strove to do it well. Abstractions became somebody else's business. Clara's illness required me to live more selflessly, and from moment to moment. Along with old lovers, nostalgia, existential worry, doubts about which road to take, I ditched fiction, writing it, reading it, thinking about it much at all. My life became non-fiction. And then came France, and our lives again were transposed into a more poetic mode. In France we managed to recover something of the sense of a life invented on the hoof, in response to landscape and atmosphere and music and books, a fantasy life, fit for the well fed and housed.

But only tragedy keeps one the parents of young children for ever. The children grew in experience and knowledge of the world. The tricks and diversions that work well for the under-tens, and even nourish them, are scarcely more useful than circus skills in adolescence. One of the consequences of choosing a Quaker school for their secondary education was that suddenly the doors were flung wide open on to not the outside world, because that was a world of sheep and hills and beehives and gardens, but the world beyond that, with all its poverty, injustice, exploitation, destitution, war, epidemics, corruption and violence. I found myself less busy wiping cut knees, or hunting for lost pieces of Playmobil, and required suddenly to explain rape and child labour and acts of terror. At the school they teach that conflict in itself is not wrong, that it is to be welcomed, as long as non-violent, non-aggressive ways of resolving it can be found. Our uneasiness about the children attending an independent school, thanks to the philanthropy of a family of enlightened industrialists, is slightly assuaged by the school's determination that pupils should emerge with a sense not of entitlement and superiority, but of humility and determination to lead ethical, socially responsible lives. Sometimes the discrepancy between aspiration and reality is very great. The child who has been properly congratulated for taking part in a run to raise money for a carbon recycler in an Indian village glances at a small boy entering the art room and says casually, audibly, to his friend, 'I hate that fucking kid.'

As I write, Ebola and the activities of ISIS are the two main stories of the first part of the year. For a few weeks after the attacks on the French satirical magazine *Charlie Hebdo*, the nature of French society, which had concerned us deeply, personally, as a family, became a subject of worldwide reflection. Friends who were teachers in France complained of the impossibility of explaining to their pupils what had happened. Teachers and parents everywhere found themselves without the vocabulary or frame of reference to talk about these things intelligently or sensitively. It was OK, just about, to say that radicalisation of individuals might be linked to the ghettoisation of Muslims in densely populated *quartiers populaires* (one of the phrases I had constantly worried over in my translations, failing ever to find anything as precise but unjudgemental in character). It was OK to say that one felt uncomfortable seeing certain heads of state walking in solidarity with a crowd of millions expressing their horror at the atrocities against writers, artists and Jews. But it was definitely not OK to say that the artists who worked on *Charlie Hebdo* had known what the price of their satirical provocations might be, and decided to go ahead anyway. I kept quiet during certain conversations, feeling that though I had lived in France for much of my adult life, and had occasionally read *Charlie*, I could not speak dispassionately because I had known, briefly, what it felt like to be an outsider, someone whose way of looking at the world was not entirely tuned to rationalism all the time, or comfortable with the neutral and prosaic secularity of the République française, and my feelings in that situation had frightened me. They frightened me now too: the horror I felt at these hideous murders was not directed at something alien and unfamiliar, but at something inside myself.

The house we live in now backs on to the Mendips, the line of hills that runs from Frome in the east to the sea south of Bristol. Edward Thomas cycled from London to the Quantocks in 1938. I like to think he passed our front door in the village high street, that a woman lived here, with her family, who was shaking out a rug as he cycled by, and wished him good-day. The garden behind the house rises through a succession of terraces to a point from which you can look out across the Somerset Levels. A chessboard of fields, divided by small tangled hedges, with what we called dykes in Lincolnshire but here are called rhynes, lime-green on the surface, past which I hurry Clara, out of habit, though the doctors say it's OK. The rivers broke their banks the year we arrived, and the farmland lay underwater for weeks. Politicians flew in by helicopter. You imagined their PAs being sent out in taxis to purchase last-minute wellies before they boarded, ducking under the rotor blades, thrusting them through the window: 'Minister, you'll be needing these!' On the ground they made promises about cutting carbon emissions, to farmers who couldn't lift their potatoes from the ground. Glastonbury Tor rises to the south-east, and other hills, Brent Knoll and Nyland and Draycott. In the days of the Knights of the Round Table, all this, the Isle of Avalon, would have been underwater. Christ walked here, they say, with his uncle, Joseph of Arimathea. Arthur and Guinevere are unmistakable presences, and Morgan le Fay. Once I wound down my car window and asked a woman in Glastonbury if I was OK to park for twenty minutes in a bay in the High Street. 'Hang on, I'll just check,' she said. She walked over to a notice: 'Yes, you're fine.' She was wearing a dark green velvet cloak and had ears that tapered to a point at the top. Some fairy friends joined her and they whooshed up the town-hall steps and into the fairy convention. At Wells Cathedral they film BBC Tudor dramas, and choristors sing by candlelight at Christmas. This is England.

When crassness, bigotry and unkindness threaten your happiness, you can run away, as we did, though not too often, but you can't avoid it altogether. You hope you and your children will not be responsible for their spread in the world. That you will be on the side of right, of the weak and oppressed who can't fight for themselves, that you will stand up to bullies and avoid vanity and pride. That you will be ready to compromise your own quality of life in the interests of people you've never met, and people who aren't yet born. You aim to teach your children not to trample on things that are precious to others, even when you don't understand them. That self-knowledge is the point of departure of all truth. That getting a highly paid job isn't the only point in acquiring an education. That good poetry says most of what we need to know. That silence, freely chosen, is the complement of free speech. That nature has enough special effects of its own. That solidarity with an unpopular minority is less comfortable and harder to maintain than solidarity with a vast majority. That lightness of being is no excuse for triviality.

They observe Earth Hour in this village with a candlelit concert in the church, and this year I will play and sing. We are busy rehearsing at weekends now, preparing for the one hour out of the 8,766 in the year when we consume no energy. There is some debate about whether we should sing and play from sheet music printed off the internet (high carbon footprint) or from iPads that glow in the dark and, for instrumentalists, can be linked to a foot pedal for page-turning via Bluetooth. I am trying to memorise Dvořák's *Humoresque*, a far cry from the *Stabat Mater*, so that I can play it without either. In his essay 'Must Classical Music Be Entirely Serious?', Alfred Brendel says: 'the pleasure one takes in laughing at a good joke is the celebration of the human mind's ability to resolve a paradox, through the act of appreciating an irony'.

Alors? I am stuck with the knowledge that my daughter's life depends on the continuing quality of her medical treatment, which comes at a cost to the state of many thousands of pounds a year. The treatments that save her life are tested on animals in laboratories. We give money to children's charities, and wear clothes produced by child labour. We eat organic vegetables, produced in the lee of the nuclear power station. We holiday at home, and use a private car because public transport is full of germs. All our aspirations, for good health, a fair world, a sustainable environment, survive inside our faulty, misshapen realities, which take different forms from generation to generation. We want a just and rational society in which our children are free to dream dreams. *Alors? Alors*, make soup. Laugh. Sing. Vote. Agitate. Be indignant. Be thankful. Walk. Watch the sky.

Akhmatova, Anna, 'The Sentence', from *Complete Poems of Anna Akhmatova*, Edinburgh: Canongate Press, 1992. Translations of Akhmatova's poetry copyright © 1989, 1992, 1997, 2000 by Judith Hemschemeyer.

Alain-Fournier, *Le Grand Meaulnes*, Paris: Livre de Poche; this translation by Helen Stevenson. See Alain-Fournier, *The Lost Domain*, London: Penguin, 1996.

Balzac, Honoré de, *La Cousine Bette*, this translation by Nico Mann. See Balzac, *Cousin Bette*, London: Penguin, 1998.

Cather, Willa, *Death Comes for the Archbishop*, London: Virago Modern Classics, 1995.

Colette, *En Pays Connu*, Paris: Ferenczi, 1950. Quoted in translation by Judith Thurman, *Secrets of the Flesh: a Life of Colette*, London: Bloomsbury 1999.

Darrieussecq, Marie, *Naissance des Fantômes*, Paris: Gallimard, 1998. See Darrieussecq, *My Phantom Husband*, London: Faber, 2000, translated by Helen Stevenson.

Dickinson, Emily, 'I Breathed Enough to Take the Trick', from *The Complete Poems* ed. Thomas H. Johnson, London: Faber and Faber, 1970.

Dinesen, Isak, *The Deluge at Nordenay*, one of *Seven Gothic Tales*, London: Penguin, 2002.

Gide, André, *Les Faux-monnayeurs*, Paris: Gallimard, 1925; this excerpt translated by Nico Mann. See Gide, *The Counterfeiters*, London: Penguin, 1990.

Huston, Nancy, *Fault Lines*, London: Atlantic, 2009.

Kenyon, Jane, 'In the Nursing Home' and 'Let Evening

Come' from *Collected Poems*. Copyright © 2005 by the Estate of Jane Kenyon. Reprinted with the permission of The Permissions Company, Inc. on behalf of Graywolf Press, Minneapolis, Minnesota, www.graywolfpress.org.

Kermode, Frank, *A Sense of an Ending*, Oxford: OUP, 2000.

Kundera, Milan, *The Unbearable Lightness of Being*, translated by Michael Henry Heim, London: Faber & Faber, 1984.

Lessing, Doris, *The Golden Notebook*, London: Grafton, 1973.

Mahy, Margaret, extracts from *A Lion in the Meadow*. Copyright © Margaret Mahy, 1969, 1986. Reprinted with the kind permission of Orion's Children's Books, part of the Hachette Children's Group, London.

Mahy, Margaret, *A Dissolving Ghost: Essays and More*, Wellington: Victoria University Press, 2000.

Mann, Sally, *Hold Still: A Memoir with Photographs*, New York: Little Brown, 2015.

Marot, Clément, '*Ma Mignonne*', from *Œuvres Complètes*, Paris: Librairie A. G. Nizet, 1977; this translation by Nico Mann.

Moberly, Miss and Jourdain, Miss, *An Adventure*, London: Faber & Faber, 1932.

Norge, Géo (Georges Mogin), '*Petite Pomme*', from *Poésies 1923–1988*, ed. Lorand Gaspar, Paris: Gallimard, 1990; this translation by Nico Mann.

Robinson, Joan G., *When Marnie Was There*, London: Collins, 2002.

Tsvetaeva, Marina: from her notebooks, quoted in *Silences* by Tillie Olsen, London: Virago, 1980.

Verlaine, Paul, '*Le Piano que Baise une Main Frêle*', from *Romances sans Paroles*, Paris: Nathan, 2012; this translation by Nico Mann.

Webster, Jean, *Daddy-Long-Legs*, London: Hodder and Stoughton, 1913.

Weil, Simone, *Leçons de Philosophie de Simone Weil (Roanne 1933–34), présentées par Anne Reynaud*, Paris: Plon,1959; this translation by Helen Stevenson.

Whitman, Walt, extract from *Leaves of Grass, Complete Poetry and Collected Prose*, New York: Literary Classics of the United States; Cambridge: Press Syndicate of the University of Cambridge, 1982.

Wild, Margaret, extract from *Remember Me*, Copyright © Margaret Wild. Reproduced by kind permission. Park Ridge, Illinois: Albert Whitman and Company, 1995.

Woolf, Virginia, *The Mark on the Wall*, London, 1917. See Woolf, *The Mark on the Wall and Other Short Fiction*, ed. D. Bradshaw, Oxford: OUP, 2008.

Woolf, Virginia, *The Diary of Virginia Woolf*, London: Hogarth Press, 1980.

My thanks and appreciation to Clare Alexander; to Donna Coonan, the perfect editor for this book, and to all the team at Virago; and to Sarah Gillespie, for allowing us to use a detail from one of her beautiful drawings, and for the inspiration of all her extraordinary work.

Particular thanks to Donald Hall for permission to reprint the poems of Jane Kenyon; also to Margaret Wild, for the extract from her remarkable picture book, *Remember Me*. This captivating and funny account of the relationship between a small girl and her increasingly forgetful and confused grandmother is currently, but I hope not permanently, out of print.

Love Like Salt was originally called *Not From Here*, and was written as a birthday present for Nico Mann. My thanks to him for allowing me to pass it on, for reading and re-reading it along the way, and for his elegant and witty translations of the French poems. Also to Beth Holgate, *ma cousine Bette*. To Clara for not minding, and for her illustrations. And finally to Verity for reminding me that 'it's just a book of stories that happen to be about us'.